INSIGHT POCKET GUIDE

Discovery CHANNEL

APA PUBLICATIONS

Part of the Langenscheidt Publishing Group

Nepal

30 km / 50 miles

Welcome!

This guidebook combines the interests and enthusiasms of two of the world's best-known information providers: Insight Guides, who have set the standard for visual travel guides since 1970, and Discovery Channel, the world's premier source of non-fiction television programming.

Locally-based author Lisa Choegyal has created a series of 22 tailor-made itineraries – on foot, bicycle or by car – to help you get to grips with this enchanting country as quickly and easily as possible. Experience the three great Durbar Squares of Kathmandu, Patan and Bhaktapur, and the famous shrines of Bodhnath, Pashupatinath and Swayambhunath; explore the less-trodden corners of the Kathmandu Valley – the distant towns of Kirtipur and Panauti, the temples of Changu Narayan and Chandeshwari, and the stupa of Namo Buddha; or take one of several excursions to the rivers, mountains and jungles outside the Kathmandu Valley. The constant action in the streets, the clarity of light and the vibrant colours of the Kathmandu Valley are almost as engaging as the character of the Nepalese people, whose rich culture and traditions are apparent everywhere you turn.

 Lisa Choegyal first came to Nepal over 25 years ago. Trekking in the Annapurnas, she became fascinated with the country and was enticed to the lowland jungles of Chitwan. 'I have lived here ever since and feel privileged that life has worked out this way for me,' she says. Choegyal now works as a director with Nepal's largest adventure travel group.

C O N T E N T S

*Pages 2/3:
forest below
Annapurna II*

*Pages 8/9:
masked dancers,
Hanuman Palace*

HISTORY & CULTURE

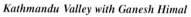

Nepal has long intrigued outsiders with fables of Lost Horizons and Shangri-Las. Shrouded in mystery until as recently as the 1950s when its borders were first opened to foreigners, Nepal has an astonishing diversity of terrain for such a small country. In just one day the organised visitor can fly amidst the world's highest mountains, browse amongst some of the most beautiful temples in the world and ride elephants in the tall grasslands of the jungles.

A landlocked rectangle that curves along the line of the central Himalaya, Nepal is 885km (553 miles) long and from 145km (90 miles) to 240km (150 miles) wide. The stupendous heights of the white Himalaya, the 'Abode of the Gods', dominate the country and its culture. Eight of the 10 highest mountains in the world are within or on Nepal's borders, including the highest, Mount Everest, at 8,848m (29,028ft).

Massive rivers plunge through Himalayan gorges as they race from the high Tibetan plateau through the Mahabharat, or middle hills, irrigating the ochre-red terraces, then slowing down through the fertile farmlands of the Terai lowlands and hardwood forests

Kathmandu Valley with Ganesh Himal

of the Siwalik (Churia) hills before eventually draining into the mighty River Ganges.

Entirely mountainous except for the narrow strip of the Terai along its southern border, Nepal's climates range from the alpine sub-zero temperatures of the highlands to the tropical heat of the Terai lowlands. Squeezed, physically and politically, between the vastness of China and India, Nepal's 23.7 million people live in a country roughly the size of England or New Zealand. They are a diverse mix of cultures and customs and nowhere can this be better appreciated than in the Kathmandu Valley.

Valley of Plenty

Situated between the Great Himalayan and the Mahabharat ranges and located almost in the centre of Nepal, the broad fertile acres of the Valley of Kathmandu is the obvious choice for its capital. Covering an area of 570 sq km (220 sq miles), the Valley today supports a population of over one and a half million people. The alluvial floor is very suitable for growing rice, the staple diet of the Nepalese, and it is well irrigated by the Bagmati River. At an altitude of 1,350m (4,400ft) above sea level, few capital cities enjoy such a clement climate with an unusual amount of sunshine and mean temperatures pleasantly varying between 10°–36°C (50°–97°F).

Pashupatinath Temple

Agriculture plays an important role in the daily life of the inhabitants and the changing cycle of the seasons is marked with the intense greens and yellows of cereal crops, the golden heaps of rice and the vivid reds of chillies. Natural wonders arrest the visitor at every turn in the Kathmandu Valley. Rivers and streams interlace the landscape, the brick-red villages cling to ridges to preserve precious land and even from the bustling centres of the cities it is possible to catch a glimpse of the snowcapped peaks of the majestic Himalaya against the intensely blue sky. The most vibrant element of all is the people of Nepal and their rich kaleidoscope of culture.

Crossroads of Culture

Nowhere in the world can one find the same concentration of culture, art and tradition that co-exist in the Kathmandu Valley. Isolated by the Himalayan barrier to the north and malarial swamps to the south, Kathmandu Valley is a crucible of culture distilled from

A Terai wedding procession

centuries of travellers, traders, artists and artisans on their way between the ancient civilisations of China and India. The diversity of the people is immediately visible in the faces of the colourfully-clad crowds who cram the medieval streets of the old cities. The richness of the heritage can be measured in the tangle of temples, shrines, stupas and palaces, each more gloriously adorned than the next.

Kathmandu is a true cultural crossroads for the more than 30 different ethnic groups who live in the hills and lowland Terai of Nepal, a mosaic that embraces both Aryan and Mongol races, several religions and as many languages and traditions as there are peoples. Besides the Sanskrit-based official language, Nepali, there are as many as 50 different languages, and many more dialects.

People come to the Kathmandu Valley on holy pilgrimages, to celebrate a special festival or to trade and barter in the bazaars. Many of the hill people still consider the Kathmandu Valley to be 'Nepal'. Thronging the streets you may see people from the north of Tibetan descent, Tamangs or 'horsemen', and the Sherpas of international mountain climbing fame. From all through the middle hills come Rais, Limbus, Gurungs Magars and Thakalis, and the ubiquitous Brahmans and Chhetris, the high caste warriors. From the Terai come the aboriginal Tharus and Majhis, and many people of Indian origin. The early inhabitants of the Kathmandu Valley, the Newars, are one of the oldest of the ethnic groups, with a language so unusual its origins are still debated.

Sealed for centuries from Westerners, a common denominator of the myriad people of Nepal is their national pride and fierce independence, derived perhaps from the fact that Nepal has never been colonised, unlike so many Asian neighbours. Politeness is rated very highly by Nepalis, and to avoid offence remember this and keep any opinions you may have on controversial or political subjects to yourself. You will see portraits everywhere of the king and, although now only a constitutional monarch, he is still highly respected in Nepal.

Every Breath a Prayer

It is easy to believe that there are more gods than people in Kathmandu. The fusion of faith found uniquely in the Valley may be theologically bewildering but it is necessary to understand something of the religion to appreciate its role in the day-to-day life of the Nepali people.

It is often hard to distinguish between the two main spiritual currents of Hinduism and Buddhism, especially when they are interwoven with the exotica of Tantrism against a background of animistic cults retained from the distant past. As a very general rule, both Hindu and Buddhist temples may take the pagoda form, the difference is that the *shikara*-style temples are Hindu and the white-dome stupas are Buddhist.

The Hindu pantheon of gods include many colourful characters and fanciful stories. Many of these gods and goddesses appear in different guises under different names, which can be confusing to the visitor. Hardly a week passes without a festival, and daily offerings of flower petals, rice and vermilion powder on a brass tray are proffered in *puja* (to renew communion with the deities particularly relevant to one's own particular problems or circumstances) at the many hundreds of different shrines. Ritual sacrifice, whether as a blessing, initiation or as part of a festival, is always performed using a male animal, invariably a chicken, goat or buffalo. Sacrifice is a cornerstone of worship in Nepal's Hindu religion.

Many of Kathmandu's Newars are Buddhist, but will recognise Hindu gods in different forms and the same is true vice versa; Hindus regard the Buddha as an incarnation of Vishnu. It has been said that if one asks a Newar if he is Hindu or Buddhist, he will reply, 'Yes'. The question is meaningless and implies an exclusive choice which is completely foreign to the scope of the Newar's religious experience. The mixing of the two religions, plus the influence of Tantrism (*see below*), has added to the proliferation of cults, deities and celebrations.

Although political leaders have always been Hindu, Buddhism since its emergence in the 6th century, has been tolerated. In the centuries following the life of the Buddha in India, many doctrinal disputes arose, leading to various schisms in the philosophy. Most important was the break between the Theravada school, which today is dominant in Southeast Asia and Sri Lanka, and the Mahayana school, which spread north to Tibet. Tibetan or Mahayana Buddhism became highly developed in the remote vastness of the Tibetan plateau where it absorbed the original shamanisitic *Bon* faith. The followers of the four main sects of Mahayana Buddhism acknowledge the Dalai Lama as their spiritual leader. Tibetan Buddhism now thrives in Nepal's atmosphere of religious tolerance. Many new monasteries have been built at Bodhnath and Swayambhunath, and Buddha's birthplace at Lumbini is being developed for viewing by visitors.

One cannot speak of religions in Nepal without touching on the practice of Tantrism, a legacy of the pre-Buddhist medieval cultures of India which has been

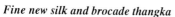

Fine new silk and brocade thangka

largely eliminated elsewhere, thanks to the Moslem conquest, the influence of the British Raj and modern secularisation. Tantra is a Sanskrit word, referring to the basic warp of threads in weaving. Literally, Tantrism reiterates the Buddhist philosophy of the essential interweaving of all things and actions. It expanded the realm of Hindu gods, cults and rites and created within Buddhism a major trend called Vajrayana, the 'Path of the Thunderbolt', which reached great importance in Nepal, often finding expression in esoteric practices. The numerous Tantric gods are represented in human and animal forms, often with multiple hands and legs symbolising the omnipresence and omnipotence of the divine. Many of these deities have a terrifying appearance, like forbidding Bhairav, blood-thirsty Kali or ambivalent Shiva, who in the Tantric pantheon is both a creator and destroyer.

With such diversity, religious tolerance within Nepal is of the essence. Over the centuries, all the masterpieces of art produced by the great civilisations of the Kathmandu Valley have been almost entirely religious in character, whether architecture, sculpture, wood-carving, metalwork, literature, music or dance. The marvellous legacy left by the early Newar artists and craftsmen is all inspired by their deities. No visitor can fail to be impressed by the wealth to be found literally lying around, the heritage of previous generations. The creative and turbulent history of the country explains many apparent conundrums.

The Legend of the Lake

In the distant dawn of unrecorded time when deities mingled with mortals the Valley of Kathmandu was a turquoise lake on which floated a white lotus flower from which emanated an awesome flame. Wishing to worship the flame more closely, the Buddhist patriarch Manjushri came from his mountain retreat in China and sliced the restraining Valley wall with his sacred sword so that the lotus might settle on what is now the hill of Swayambhunath.

A Hindu version of the story is that Krishna released the waters by hurling a thunderbolt at the Valley wall. Whatever the fiction, geologists confirm that the Kathmandu Valley was once under water and the Chobar gorge is not only as narrow as a blade but below it, enshrined in a temple, is a stone that some believe to be Krishna's thunderbolt.

The evocative mythology of early Nepal gradually dissolves as, after several successive waves of hazy Tibeto-Burman migrants, the dynasty of Kirati kings gradually comes into historic focus in the seventh or eighth century BC. These apparently fierce tribal people invaded from the east and may have been the Kiriaths of Old Testament Babylon. Buddha was born as Prince Siddhartha Gautama in Lumbini in south Nepal during the reign of the 28 Kirati kings – the actual date of 543BC is disputed. Two centuries later the great Indian emperor Ashoka embraced Buddhism and converted his empire. He visited Lumbini, raised the engraved column and is believed to have visited the Kathmandu Valley and had the Ashoka stupas built in Patan, though there is no actual proof of this.

Licchavi Legacy

When the Kiratis had succumbed to the Licchavi invasion from India in about AD300, the first golden age of Nepalese art flourished: stone sculptures survive today as a testament to the skill of their craftsmen. The oldest inscription in the Valley, AD464, is etched on a stone pillar at Changu Narayan, confirming King Manadeva I as a monarch of considerable talents, responsible for expanding his empire both to the east and west. The Licchavis also laid down the hierarchical structure of Nepalese society, according to the Hindu caste system.

The three Thakuri dynasties began in AD602 with the ascent of King Amsuvarman, who married his sister to an Indian prince and his daughter, Bhrikuti, to Tibet's powerful King Tsrong-tsong Gompo. Bhrikuti is believed to have taken, as part of her dowry, the begging bowl of the Buddha. Her role in converting Tibet to Buddhism has made her a legendary figure, reincarnated as the Green Tara.

The Thakuri dynasties inaugurated the three great festivals of Indrajatra, Krishna Jayanti and the Machhendranath Jatras and it was during their time that the Kasthamandap or 'Pavilion of Wood' was constructed from a single tree, giving Kathmandu its name. This period lasted until 1200 and is termed Nepal's 'Dark Ages', as so little else is known of this time of obscure turmoil.

Marvellous Mallas (1274–1769)

The Malla kings controlled Nepal from the 13th to 18th centuries during a predominantly stable age of peace and plenty. It was the Malla kings who established the custom of being considered incarnations of Vishnu, as are the present Shah rulers. They adopted the Taleju Bhawani from South India as the royal goddess of Nepal. Although they were strict Hindus, they were tolerant of Buddhism which was widespread among the people, especially in its Tantric form. They developed the familiar compact villages seen today in the Valley, using brick and tiles for the first time and clustered

King Bupathindra Malla at Bhaktapur

together to preserve and cultivate limited arable land and as protection against bandits.

The Mallas survived an unsettled period of earthquakes and the brief Moslem invasion of 1336. By the early 15th century they had introduced Newari as the court language and chosen Bhaktapur as their capital. A renaissance of art and culture flourished, laying the foundations of what we see today.

The dividing of the Valley in 1482 into three separate kingdoms, Kathmandu, Patan (Lalitpur) and Bhaktapur (Bhadgaon), no doubt encouraged each to compete with the next to glorify their palaces and temples, but led eventually to the downfall of their dynasty.

Shah Supremacy (1723–1846)

Political rivalries amongst the divided city-states led to their demise. The opportunity was seized by the king of Gorkha, then a principality situated halfway between Kirtipur and Pokhara, and which had been growing in strength under the dynamic leadership of King Prithvi Narayan Shah. After 10 years of preparation from his fort at Nuwakot, the founder of modern Nepal took Kathmandu and Patan by force in 1768 and Bhaktapur and Kirtipur yielded to him in 1769 by trickery and intrigue. The Valley was unified and he established Kathmandu as his capital. King Prithvi Narayan Shah and his descendants consolidated and expanded the new empire until it stretched from Kashmir to Sikkim, double its present size.

This led to inevitable conflicts with neighbours and the Chinese were eventually called in by the Tibetans to curb Nepal's expansionist ambitions to the north. An agreement was reached in 1792 which forced Nepal to desist.

A full-scale war with British India lasted from 1814 to 1816 and ended in the Treaty of Friendship, signed at Segauli, which shrank the borders to their present size and established a permanent British presence in Kathmandu. Brian Hodgeson was not the first European to visit the fabled Valley. The first British envoy, William Kirkpatrick, had visited in 1792 with regard to the disputes with Tibet, and the Italian Capuchins had been permitted a mission as early as 1730.

There is an interesting footnote to this period. The gallantry the Gorkha soldiers displayed in the 1816 conflict so impressed the British that they enlisted them into the British Indian Army. Even today the Gurkhas, as they are now called, are recognised as outstanding soldiers by the British and Indians.

Rana Rule (1846–1951)

In 1846, taking advantage of palace intrigues, the Kot Massacre was staged by the shrewd and enterprising Jung Bahadur Rana, who designated himself as prime minister, and later 'maharajah', with powers superior to those of the sovereign. He made his office hereditary, establishing a unique line of succession that went first to brothers and only then to sons. Ruthlessly suppressing all opposition,

A Kathmandu monument

he took the highly unusual step of travelling to Europe and was much impressed with Queen Victoria and the fashions of the day. On his return, he launched a frivolous vogue of neo-classical palaces, and ladies of the court arranged their *saris* to look like crinolines.

In all other respects, however, travel remained limited to a privileged few and foreigners were treated with extreme distrust.

It was only after King Tribhuvan managed, with India's help, to regain power in the almost-bloodless coup of early 1951 that Nepal opened its doors to the outside world. In 1953 Edmund Hillary and Sherpa Tenzing Norgay climbed Mount Everest – the news reached London on the eve of Queen Elizabeth's coronation. In the next decade the 'hippies' discovered the joys of the Valley and settled in – until revised visa laws sent them on their way.

Despite early intentions, it was not until 1959 that Tribhuvan's son, King Mahendra, established a constitution that provided for a parliamentary system of government. The first general election in Nepal's history took place over several months in that year but the experiment with democracy was short-lived and ended in 1960 with the king taking back power. The 1962 constitution established the *panchayat* system, an administrative and legislative system culminating in an indirectly-elected national legislature, with the prime minister and Cabinet appointed by the king.

King Mahendra died in 1972, and was succeeded by his son, the youthful King Birendra, who declared as his goal the improvement of the standard of living of his people. A referendum in 1980 reconfirmed the people's support of the monarchy and King Birendra, but by April 1990 popular dissatisfaction with the lack of reforms and corrupt officials erupted into demonstrations and riots in Kathmandu. The ban on the multi-party system was lifted, a democratic constitution was announced in November 1990 and a general election held in May 1991.

Nepal Today

King Birendra Bir Bikram Shah Dev is constitutional monarch of the only Hindu kingdom in the world, and at the start of the 21st century his country is faced with problems of Himalayan size. Nepal's first decade of democracy has been characterised by political instability with short-lived coalitions and changing prime ministers. The population is increasing at an annual rate of 2.5 percent and rural poverty remains the chief problem. Foreign aid is a large component in Nepal's development budget and the nation's precarious position as a Himalayan buffer state between India and China may still be its best guarantee of survival, a foreign policy unchanged for centuries.

Historical Highlights

8th century BC–AD300 The history of the eastern Kirati kings are inextricably interwoven with legend.

AD300–700 The first golden age of Nepalese arts flourish in the Licchavi dynasty. The Valley's earliest stone inscription describes Nepal's first great historical figure, King Manadeva I. Leaving a legacy of superb stone sculptures, the Licchavis instigate the tradition of a hierarchical Hindu caste society.

AD602–1200 The 'Dark Ages' of turmoil under the Thakuris, probably from northern India. Princess Bhrikuti of Nepal marries King Tsrong-tsong Gompo of Tibet and is deified as the Green Tara for converting him and Tibet to Buddhism, along with her Chinese co-wife, the White Tara.

1200 King Arideva assumes the title Malla, and sets up a new, highly-accomplished dynasty. The Mallas bring riches and recognition to Nepal, reinforce the caste system and establish the villages familiar to us today.

1336 The Mallas survive a raid by the Sultan of Bengal. By the 15th century a renaissance flourishes and many great buildings, fine woodcarving and powerful sculpture seen today belong to this period.

1482 King Yaksha Malla dies; the Valley is divided and ruled as three city-states: Kathmandu, Patan (Lalitpur) and Bhaktapur (Bhadgaon). Agriculture and cottage industries thrive but political rivalries fragment the empire.

1768 Prithvi Narayan Shah, ruler of Gorkha, conquers Kathmandu and Patan and takes Bhaktapur a year later, thus founding a united Nepal and the present Shah dynasty. Expansionist policies and conflicts of trading interests lead to clashes with Nepal's neighbours.

1792 Invasion by Chinese troops follows several wars with Tibet. Nepal has to pledge to desist from attacking Tibet and to pay tribute regularly to the Chinese emperor in Peking.

1816 'Treaty of Friendship' signed; ends two years of war with British India. Nepal's territory is cut in half to its present borders. A British representative is established in Kathmandu, the first and only Western envoy resident in Nepal.

1846 Jung Bahadur Rana takes advantage of palace intrigue to stage the 'Kot Massacre' and establishes the Rana regime of hereditary ruling prime ministers. The Ranas rule Nepal, virtually keeping the royal family prisoners for ceremonial and religious purposes.

1951 King Tribhuvan regains royal power, aided by recently independent India. Foreigners are now allowed into Nepal and two years later, Mount Everest is climbed.

1962 After an unsuccessful experiment with parliamentary rule, King Mahendra institutes the *panchayat* system of government.

1972 King Birendra succeeds to the throne on the death of his father, King Mahendra.

1980 A national referendum is called by King Birendra following unrest, and reaffirms the people's confidence in the *panchayat* system.

1990 Following demonstrations and riots, King Birendra on 8 April lifts the legal ban on political parties. The constitution of 9 November invests sovereignty in the people, guarantees human rights and introduces a parliamentary system with the king relegated to the status of a constitutional monarch.

1991 The general election on 12 May is won by the Nepali Congress and Girija Prasad Koirala becomes Prime Minister.

1991–2000 First decade of democracy characterised by short-lived coalitions and frequent changes of prime minister.

Kathmandu Valley

4 km / 2.5 miles

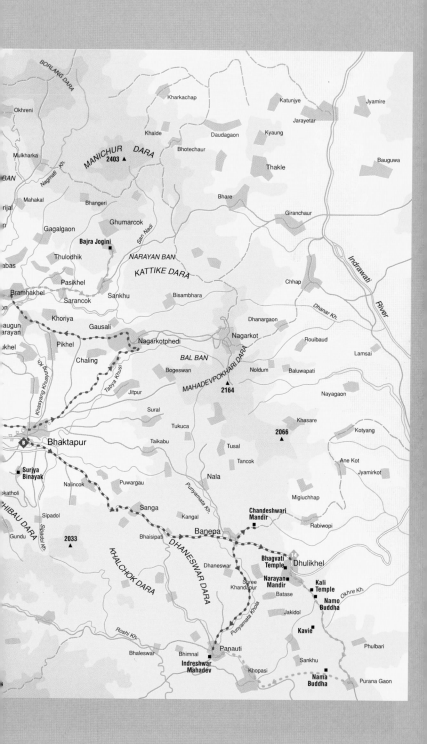

Day Itineraries

Everyone arriving in Kathmandu is exhilarated by the sparkling views, the friendly people and often the thrill of being in a city of which they have long dreamed. These first three days are designed to crystalise that excitement.

DAY 1

Kathmandu Durbar Square and Bodhnath

Wander in the medieval magic of the Kathmandu Durbar Square. Walk through the bazaars of Asan and Indrachowk. Lunch at the Tukche Thakali Kitchen on Durbar Marg. Grab a cab to Chabahil and linger at the stupa of Bodhnath, then drive through the countryside to the Gokarna Mahadev temple.

Looking west across the Kathmandu Valley

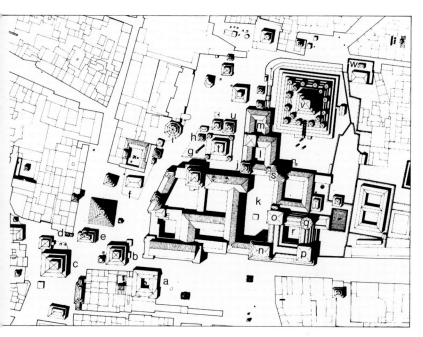

Although Nepalis live with the light, the morning mist in the winter makes it pointless leaving your hotel until 9.30am, after a leisurely breakfast. Spring and early autumn are more inspiring for an early start.

From the **Tundhikhel**, the central parade ground that separates the new city from the old, walk under the arch and up **New Road**, so-called as it was rebuilt after the terrible earthquake of 1934. It is lined with shops selling imported goods and jewellery but they do not open early.

At the top you enter a different world. On your left is forgotten **Freak Street**, the abandoned hangout of the 1960s hippies and flower children, and nearby is the raised brick platform of **Basantapur Square**, formerly the home of royal elephants.

Ahead is the **Kathmandu Durbar Square**, the hub of the old city at the crossroads of diagonal trade routes. Founded by the Licchavi kings in the 8th century, this profusion of over 50 temples and monuments is a living museum to the glorious Malla dynasty architecture, with some additions by King Prithvi Narayan Shah and the Ranas.

You first encounter the **Kumari Bahal**

Kathmandu Durbar Square

(a) Kumari Bahal
(b) Temple of Narayan
(c) Kasthamandap
(d) Ashok Binayak
(e) Shiva Temple
(f) Shiva-Parvati
     Temple House
(g) King Pratap Malla
(h) Degu Taleju Temple
(i) Basantapur Tower
(j) Hanuman Dhoka
(k) Nasal Chowk
(l) Mohan Chowk
(m) Sundari Chowk
(n) Basantapur Tower
(o) Kirtipur Tower
(p) Lalitpur Tower
(q) Bhaktapur Tower
(r) Lohan Chowk
(s) Pancha Mukhi
     Hanuman
(t) Jagnnath Temple
(u) Gopinath Mandir
(v) Taleju Temple
(w) Tarana Devi Mandir

Kathmandu

400 m / 440 yds

Royal Palace window

on the left, the mid 18th-century temple of the **Kumari** or Living Goddess. The inner façades, like the main one, have beautifully carved windows and it is here that she can sometimes be persuaded to appear to her admirers. A virgin chosen from the Sakya clan of goldsmiths, the Kumari never leaves the sanctuary of her temple except when she is ceremoniously paraded in her chariot at the festival of Indrajatra, when even the king pays her homage.

Ahead, the **Kasthamandap** is at the entrance of the **Maru Tol**, the original Pavilion of Wood said to have been constructed from a single sacred tree, and from where Kathmandu gets its name. Originally a community centre it is now a temple dedicated to Gorakhnath. Pause at the golden **Maru Ganesh** (Ashok Binayak) shrine, a monument of great importance and always very busy with devotees ensuring their safety before leaving on a journey. Rest on the nine steps of the **Shiva Temple** whilst admiring the crudely carved deities surveying the scene from the window of the **Shiva-Parvati Temple House**.

As you leave the main square, note the great drums on your left which are beaten during the worship of the **Degu Taleju** in her temple opposite. The north-facing door is panelled in silver and the 28-m (92-ft) high roof is capped with a very fine pinnacle. The proud statue of **King Pratap Malla**, who is responsible for much of this glory, is set high on a pillar opposite. Before you move on, notice the large golden mask of **Bhairav** erected in 1796, normally kept screened from view except during the festival of Indrajatra when *chhang* or local beer pours from his mouth and down the throats of the excited crowd.

This second part of the square is dominated by the towering **Taleju Temple**, dedicated to the royal deity, whose inner sanctum can only be entered by the king. Built in 1564 by Mahendra Malla, this temple used to be the highest structure in Kathmandu at 37m (121ft): it was considered inauspicious to build any higher.

Kathmandu Durbar Square at dusk

Vishnu as half-lion, half-man

The entrance to the sprawling old Royal Palace, the **Hanuman Dhoka Durbar**, is a brightly painted gate (Wednesday to Monday 10.30am–4pm; closes 2pm on Friday), flanked by awesome-looking stone lions and guarded by the palace's namesake Hanuman, the monkey god, a red-smeared image which dates from 1672. Pass through the golden doors. There is much to explore within this series of superb courtyards, beautifully decorated with woodcarving, and still used by the royal family for ceremonies and special days.

Orient yourself from the nine-storey **Basantapur Tower**. The **Kirtipur Tower** has a domed copper roof, the **Bhaktapur Tower** is of an octagonal form and the **Lalitpur Tower** overlooks New Road. The towers were named after the towns that donated and built them in recognition of the unification of Nepal by King Prithvi Narayan Shah. There are three small museums in the palace, dedicated to kings Birendra, Mahendra and Tribhuvan. The Hanuman Dhoka Durbar

was extensively restored by UNESCO for King Birendra's coronation in February 1975, delayed to coincide with this auspicious day.

Leaving behind these great marvels of art and architecture, return to the square and turn right past the fearsome features of the much revered **Black Bhairav**, and shudder at the bloodshed in the **Kot**, the armoury where Jung Bahadur enacted his merciless coup in 1846 by murdering most of those in power. The half-buried **Garuda** statue at the entrance to **Makhantol** is evocative of former times and street levels. Leaving the Durbar Square, the road narrows through the bazaar heading in a northeasterly direction. There are many shrines, courtyards and shops to investigate as you jostle with colourfully-costumed people and honking rickshaws.

At **Indrachowk**, detour into the quaint **Bead Market** through the smallest of passages behind the house opposite the many-balconied shrine to **Akash Bhairav**. Sitting in their adjacent booths, the shopkeepers will twist and string together a bewildering array of multi-coloured glass beads to your specifications.

At the next junction, **Kheltol**, step left through a small gate which leads you into the important **Seto Machhendranath Temple**, home of the guardian deity of Kathmandu, before continuing to the throng of **Asantol**. Be prepared for your senses to be bombarded with sights, sounds and smells. Keep walking straight ahead and you emerge from the bazaar at a square pond, **Rani Pokhari**, with a domed Shiva shrine in the middle. This was built in 1670 by King Pratap Malla to console his queen on the death of their son.

Cross the road, but not before noting where you can rent a bicycle, and head along **Jamaltol** to **Durbar Marg**, the wide avenue where most of the travel agents and airlines are to be found. The **Narayan Hiti Royal Palace** (open daily 10am–5pm) is in front of you, named after the water spout found at the top of the street on the right.

Indrachowk

Half-way up Durbar Marg, on the left, is the **Tukche Thakali Kitchen** (tel: 01-225890), a delightful little restaurant that makes an interesting stop for lunch. The Thakalis come from the Annapurna region and are renowned for their hospitality, running some of the best tea houses and lodges in Nepal. To help those who do not know what to choose from the menu, there are set meals. Watch out for the fiery local brandy, which is somewhat of an acquired taste.

When you feel refreshed, take a taxi or better still, arrange a hired car and head north past the Royal Palace up **Lazimpat** and **Maharajgunj**, the area where many foreign missions are found, past the two Princes' palaces to **Ring Road**, which circles the city. This is not the most direct route to Bodhnath but it gives you a chance to gauge the size of the city and appreciate its rural nature. On a clear day the white peaks of **Ganesh Himal** and **Dorje Lakpa** can be seen across the rice fields and distant foothills.

Bodhnath Stupa

It is worth stopping at the stupa of **Chabahil**, one of the very earliest settlements in the Valley, now sitting rather dilapidated. Chabahil stupa is said to have been constructed from materials left over from Bodhnath. To the west about 200m (215yds) is the beautiful Ganesh shrine of **Chandra Binayak** which is believed to cure diseases and injuries. A brass shrew waits for Ganesh, the helpful son of Shiva, atop a pillar in front of the shrine, resplendent under a modern light. For those in need of refreshment, the new Hyatt Regency Hotel nearby has a pool, restaurants and bars.

Spend time lingering at **Bodhnath Stupa**, the largest temple of its kind in the whole of Nepal, whose great dome rises out of the paddy fields against a brilliant blue sky with a backdrop of white Himalayan peaks. Shaped like a massive *mandala*, which is best discerned from the air, and decorated with strings of fluttering prayer flags, Bodhnath has always been a centre for trade with Tibet. The all-seeing eyes on the stupa follow the Buddhist pilgrims who have come from Tibet, Ladakh, Bhutan and the northern parts of Nepal as they circumambulate clockwise, spinning the embossed prayer wheels. Along the base of the great hemispherical stupa is a ring of 108 small inset images of the Buddha.

To get a glimpse of Buddhist life, explore the surrounding monasteries, many of which are newly built by Western as well as local donors. Bodhnath has become one of the most important Tibetan Buddhist centres in the world.

A charming legend obscures the ancient origins of Bodhnath. It is said that a girl called Kangma built the stupa. Having been banished from heaven by Indra for stealing flowers, she was reborn, as punishment, the daughter of a swineherd. On earth she had four children, was widowed, then managed to make a fortune as a goose girl. She asked the king to give her as much land as the hide of a buffalo would cover, so that she could build a noble temple to the Buddha. The king agreed and the clever girl cut the hide into thin strips, joined them and stretched them out to encircle the land on which Bodhnath now stands.

Do not miss the shopping at the stalls and small shops that surround the stupa – trinkets, carpets and ethnic fabrics. Look out for the special little shop selling jackets and waistcoats made from the wool cloth normally used by monks and trimmed with ribbon. You may want to stop for a drink or some vegetarian food at Stupa View Restaurant.

Drive on and when the forest of Gokarna comes into sight, turn left and follow the road that winds through the fields on its way to **Sundarijal**, one of the Valley's main water supplies. After about 5km (3 miles) you reach the little village of Gokarna.

The **Gokarna Mahadev** is on the right of the road, a beautifully restored triple-roofed shrine on the banks of the sacred Bagmati with superbly carved roof struts. This was the first renovation project of the Kathmandu Valley Preservation Trust. At the **Gokarna Aunshi** festival in June or July, devotees whose fathers have died in the past year must come here and ritually bathe in the river. A particularly fine image of Parvati, Shiva's consort, is enshrined at the northwest corner, recently modestly garbed to shield her beauty.

After relaxing at your hotel, dine Nepali in grand style at **Baithak** (tel: 01-253337) at Baber Mahal Revisited. In the long gallery, past Ranas stare down from the paintings lining the walls. If you'd prefer Western food there are several other good restaurants in the area.

Bhaktapur to Panauti

Drive to the ancient city of Bhaktapur, then walk through the Durbar Square, the Taumadhi Square with the five-roofed Nyatapola Temple and the Dattatreya Square before driving on outside the Valley to the Dhulikhel Mountain Resort for lunch with a view. Return to Banepa and the Chandeshwari temple, with its extraordinary fresco of Bhairav. Finally, visit the classic Newar town of Panauti and its important temples.

Bhairav temple from the Nyatapola steps

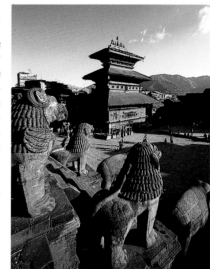

Take a taxi for the day and drive to **Bhaktapur**, also known by its old name of Bhadgaon. Leave it at the entrance to the **Durbar Square**. Foreign visitors must pay an entrance charge here. The most charming of the three squares, Durbar Square has the best preserved, 'medieval' character. Immediately evident, however, is its relative sparseness compared to squares in Kathmandu and Patan, due to the destruction caused by the 1934 earthquake.

Opposite the gilded copper **Sun Dhoka** (Golden Gate), erected in 1753 and hailed as one of the greatest single pieces of Nepali art, is the lovely statue of **Bhupatindra Malla** on his tall pillar of stone. Passing through the gate, walk left into the **Mul Chowk** and explore as far as you can before being stopped by guards from entering the sacred and richly ornamented **Taleju Chowk** and **Kumari Chowk**. You are permitted to see the sunken bathing pool known as the **Nag Pokhari**, with its beautiful gilded water spout.

Returning to the main square, notice the octagonal pavilion, the **Chayasilin Mandap**, toppled in 1934, which took three painstaking years to reconstruct – from contemporary drawings – on its original plinth. Steel girders support the exquisite woodcarving.

Adjacent to the Sun Dhoka is the **Royal Palace of 55 Windows**,

Bhaktapur (Bhadgaon)

400 m / 440 yds

Decorated torana

also rebuilt after the earthquake. Examine the sadly over-restored **thangkas** in the **National Art Gallery** (open Wednesday to Monday 10.30am–3.30pm). This is in another part of the palace located through a gateway flanked by Hanuman and Narsingh, the man-lion. Before you leave, note the **Sundari Chowk**, the ritual bathing courtyard of the Bhaktapur kings. It used to be surrounded by buildings, but is now open to the elements.

Leave by the **Taumadhi Tol**, a narrow street leading down to the **Taumadhi Square**, lined with tempting shops selling thangkas, puppets and artefacts. On your left is the superb five-roofed **Nyatapola Temple** on its five plinths, one of the tallest in the Valley over 30m (98ft) high, dedicated to a mysterious Tantric goddess. Notice the pairs of guardians who flank the main staircase, each ten times stronger than the one below. Thus the Malla wrestlers on the bottom plinth are ten times as strong as ordinary men but only one tenth as powerful as the elephants above them, and so on. It is told that King Bupathindra Malla himself carried bricks for the building of the temple to inspire the locals.

At right angles is the earlier **Kasi Bishwanath Temple**, whose Bhairav is paraded at the frenetic annual Bisket festival at the Nepali New Year. Pause for a cup of Nepali *chiya* (tea brewed together with milk, sugar and spices) in the temple cafe and enjoy the busy life of the Square. The black saris

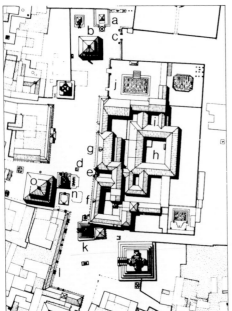

Bhaktapur Durbar Square
(a) gateway
(b) Rameshwar Temple dedicated to Shiva
(c) Temple dedicated to Durga
(d) Bhupatindra Malla
(e) Sun Dhoka
(f) Royal Palace
(g) National Art Gallery
(h) Taleju Chowk
(i) Kumari Chowk
(j) Sundari Chowk
(k) Dharmasala
(l) Tadhunchen Bahal
(m) Batsala Durga
(n) Pashupati Temple

edged in red are unique to the Newar women of Bhaktapur. Notice the *jyapus*, the Newari farmers, carrying their loads in two baskets strung on a pole across their shoulders. Only Newars use this method of carrying, all the other people of Nepal prefer to use the *doko*, or basket, supported on their backs by a strap around their foreheads.

Detour south from here, if you wish, to the **Pottery Market**, then return and walk on down the brick paved streets, via the **Golmadi Tol**, past the little **Golmadi Ganesh Shrine** to the eastern part of Bhaktapur and the **Dattatraya Square**.

Dhulikhel Mountain Resort

The **Dattatraya Temple** is the oldest in this area, as can be devised from its squat shape, not dissimilar to the Kasthamandap in Kathmandu. Considered to be one of the most important temples in the Valley, and serving as both a place of rest and a shrine, the front part (added later) houses the images of Dattatraya, honoured as Shiva's teacher.

Down a side alley behind is the famed (though somewhat overrated) **Peacock Window**. Nearby in the ancient priests' house and pilgrim hostel, the **Pujari Math**, is a **Woodcarving Museum.** It is sadly neglected, but it's worth going in to see the exquisite wood adornments in the courtyard and windows. Have the taxi meet you behind the **Nava Durga**, a rather sinister and highly revered temple that is the focus of the ritual masked dancing during festivals.

It is a very pleasant 45-minute drive through the countryside to the **Dhulikhel Mountain Resort** (tel: 011-61466) for lunch on the road to Tibet. As you leave the Valley at the village of **Sanga**, pause to look back at the panoramic view. The resort is several miles on past the town of Dhulikhel, but do not be tempted to stop at any of the other hostelries. At the Dhulikhel Mountain Resort, perched high above the road, ask to eat outside in the garden to enjoy the mountain views. If you are filled with energy, walk along the ridge for an hour or so above the resort to the little shrine beneath a big tree.

From Dhulikhel drive back down the road to Kathmandu and turn right (north) at the statue of King Tribhuvan in the middle of **Banepa**, a thriving town with many new buildings. Follow the road right and you will see the **Banepa Adventist Hospital**. Old clothes, medicines and donations are made excellent use of in this busy general hospital which serves an impressively large area.

Drive a little further – as far as you can in fact – until the golden roof of the **Chandeshwari Mandir** comes into view on the edge of a steep gorge. The forest above here was believed to have been once full of fearsome demon beasts, and the goddess Parvati was called

Brahmayani Temple, Panauti

upon to slay their leader, Chand. The shrine was built in her honour and called after her: "the Slayer of Chand". In the inner sanctum there is a fine image of Chandeshvari, but what really makes the trip worthwhile is the multi-coloured fresco of Bhairav.

Returning to the Banepa crossroads, the classic Newar town of **Panauti** is a 20-minute drive straight across, a settlement which is possibly pre-Licchavi in origin and a thriving trading town in Malla times. Leave the car at the confluence of the **Pungamati River** and visit the exquisite **Brahmayani Temple**. Cross by the suspension foot bridge and explore the scenic melange of ancient temples and *ghats*. There is a Krishna temple and several Shiva **lingums**.

Walk right to the magnificent **Indreshwar Mahadev**, one of the oldest existing temple structures with some of the earliest woodcarving to be found in Nepal. Founded as early as the 12th and 13th centuries, the carved wood roof struts are masterly in their elegant simplicity. The earthquake damage suffered in 1988 was restored by a French project. Inside its walled courtyard, note the **Narayan Temple** opposite. Panauti is the end of your walk in *Itinerary 14, Pick & Mix (page 58)*.

From Panauti it is less than an hour's journey back to Kathmandu. Indian kebabs, curries and sitar music at **Ghar-e-Kabab** (tel: 01-221711) on Durbar Marg may appeal this evening. The other top Indian restaurant in Kathmandu is **Bukhara** (tel: 01-272550) at the Hotel Soaltee Crowne Plaza. Also at this hotel is the **Al Fresco**, if you'd prefer Italian cuisine.

A Walk to Changu Narayan

An early start by car via Thimi to Nagarkot, high on the rim of the Valley. Walk for about three hours part way down the hill along a ridge with views across the Valley, picnicking en route, to the wonderful temple of Changu Narayan. Ancient sculptures litter the courtyard and here is the earliest inscription in the Valley. An evening stroll in Chetrapati and dinner in Thamel.

After an early breakfast, this morning you should leave by 8.30am in a taxi for Nagarkot (up to 2,200m/7,200ft). Take something warm

Nagarkot

to wear, a packed lunch and a water bottle. Enjoy the old back road via **Thimi**, where the terracotta animals are sold by the road-side. Look out for the particularly engaging painted figures of the king and queen. Turn off left behind Bhaktapur, past the 'industrial estate' which produces glazed pottery and handmade paper for cards sold in many shops in Kathmandu.

The road to **Nagarkot** winds upward through fields and then through pine trees, and you can feel the temperature dropping as you climb. Identify the ridge along which you will be walking later by picking out the gold roofs of Changu Narayan on the left. The view of the receding tiers of blue-grey hills culminating in the white snows will be rewarding enough for the one-hour drive. If the weather is really overcast, do not bother going to the top.

Leave the car half way down the hill at the saddle where the ridge joins the road, making sure the driver understands where to meet you – by the tea shop on the Sankhu Road below Changu. The first 20 minutes up through a pine plantation to the crest is the only uphill climb of the day. The walk is a leisurely, three-hour stroll along the ridge line with stunning views across the Valley to the high mountains. If you need reassurance, there is always someone to ask the way. Note the traces of an old Rana

Thimi pottery

irrigation system and the orange pumpkins and red chillies drying on the roofs. The glittering pinnacles of Changu Narayan tempt you on through charming Chhetri and Gurung villages. It is more peaceful to eat your picnic by the trail before you reach the village of Changu.

At the top of the main street is the superb temple complex of **Changu Narayan**, rebuilt in 1702 but with the Valley's earliest inscription etched on a pillar and dating its origins to AD464. Marvel at the treasury of priceless Licchavi sculptures of Vishnu and Garuda images, the statues of Bupathindra Malla in a gilded cage and the unusual brickwork on the platform. Changu Narayan has been designated a World Heritage Site. Kathmandu Valley has the distinction of having the largest concentration of World Heritage Sites to be found in the world. Leave by the west door of this extraordinary and important place. Now descend down a well-worn path and head for the Manohara River through which you may find you have to wade unless you can find a makeshift bridge to cross. Negotiate the paddy fields to where your taxi will be waiting beside a cluster of houses and a little tea shop.

After adjourning to your hotel to freshen up, enjoy an early evening wander, starting at the Crystal Hotel at the top of New Road and walking as straight as you can through the maze of the bazaar area. Look up to catch faces at carved windows and the lilt of an evening song.

Detour right to the **Mahabuddha Stupa** and the evening surgery of the famous ayurvedic Doctor Mana Bajracharya – ask anyone where to find his courtyard. Pass some crumbling classic *bahals*, or courtyards, and soon you reach the upbeat area of **Chetrapati** and **Thamel**, a gathering place for world travellers with lodges, trekking shops, restaurants, bars and loud music. Stop for a beer or a Khukri rum and coke – and some fascinating people-watching – at **Tom and Jerry's** or **Rum Doodle**.

There are numerous places to eat in this area but if you'd prefer local delicacies in a splendid setting take a taxi to Hotel Dwarika's **Krishnarpan Restaurant** (tel: 01-470770), where they serve excellent Newari cuisine. Otherwise, your best bet in Thamel is probably **Kilroy's** (tel: 01-250440), with an Irish chef and an interesting mix of international cuisine. Above the entrance to the restaurant are the offices of the **Kathmandu Environmental Education Project (KEEP)**, a centre for trekkers (open 10am to 5pm off season (summer/winter) and 9am to 7pm peak season (autumn/spring; tel: 01-259567, www.keepnepal.org, email keep@info.com.np).

Also here is the **Himalayan Rescue Association (HRA)**, a non-profit organisation founded in 1973 in order to save lives by alerting trekkers and mountaineers to the dangers of altitude sickness. There's a useful information centre here with a library and noticeboard. In the trekking season there are regular lectures which are worth attending (open from 10am–5pm; tel: 01-262746, email: hra@aid-post.mos.com.np).

Right, Swayambhunath stupa

PICK & MIX

These half days are deliberately designed to allow time to wander, look and absorb. If you find them too leisurely, keep moving and combine three in one day. Except where specified, these suggestions are suitable for both mornings and afternoons. You are encouraged to improvise and deviate from these itineraries, but one sight you should not miss is the superb Patan Museum.

1. Palaces of Patan

Explore the Durbar Square then walk to the Golden Temple, Kumbeshwar Temple and Mahabuddha.

Take a taxi to **Patan**, cradle of traditional arts and architecture in the Valley, which is also known by its ancient name of Lalitpur, the Beautiful City. The **Patan Durbar Square** is in the very heart of the city and must rank as one of the finest urban streetscapes in

Gilded metalwork is a feature of Patan

Golden door of Mani Keshar Chowk, Patan Museum

the world. Visit the courtyards of the **Royal Palace**, more accessible than their Kathmandu counterparts.

The present palace structure was built in the 17th century on earlier foundations. The first courtyard, the **Sundari Chowk**, the royal living quarters, was finished in 1627. It contains the spectacular **Tusha Hiti**, the royal bathing tank with a water spout in the form of a gilded conch shell. Lined with hundreds of deities of stone and metal and in an octagonal form to emphasise the king's devotion to the eight *nagas* or serpents, the perimeter of the sunken tank is guarded by a pair of dragons carved in stone.

The entrance to the Sundari Chowk is through a very narrow doorway, to the left of a more impressive entrance which is never used as it is believed to be controlled by an evil spirit. The next courtyard, the **Mul Chowk**, was completed in 1666, and has the gilded sanctuary of the **Bidya Mandir** shrine in its centre. Another favourite house goddess of the Malla kings is enshrined in the south wing of the courtyard, guarded by life-size gilded bronze figures. The **Taleju Temple** is in the north-eastern corner, and can only be entered by her priests. Note the fine doorway, a tribute to the metalworking castes for which Patan is still famous.

Next is the temple of **Degutalle**, and then the third courtyard, the **Mani Keshar Chowk**, now housing the splendid new **Patan Museum** (open Wednesday to Monday 10am–5pm, Friday closes at 3pm). The exhibits are well displayed to give visitors an excellent introduction to the beliefs and traditions of Hinduism and Buddhism. Pause in the garden for lunch at the **Patan Museum Café**. Restored in a joint Nepali-Austrian project, the building has superb exterior decoration and a lovely central gilded window from where the kings would look out over their subjects and gaze upon the magnificent **Krishna Mandir** opposite. The octagonal *shikara*-style Krishna Mandir, considered the finest stone temple in the Valley, is faced by a *garuda* on a column. Pause to enjoy the friezes depicting the epics that run clockwise around the building, rather like a cartoon strip. Adjacent to the Krishna Mandir is the **Bishwarnath Mandir**, guarded by two huge stone elephants. It is one of the earlier temples in the square and is famous for its finely carved wood pillars.

Beyond is one of the most important temples, the **Bhimsen Mandir**, sacred to Bhimsen, the god of traders, and especially worshipped by the businessmen of Patan. From the centre of the top of the three-tiered roof falls a metal ribbon-like banner engraved with mantras, donated by a wealthy benefactor.

Directly opposite, the lotus-shaped **Mangal Hiti** has three stone waterspouts in the shape of crocodile heads. This Licchavi water conduit dates from the 10th century and is now well below street level. Stand back to admire the palace façades. Return to see some interesting monuments at the upper end of the Durbar Square. **Siddhi Narasinha Malla** surveys the glory he has created from the top of his stone pillar, protected by a golden *naga* or serpent. Two-tiered **Char Narayan Mandir** was built in 1566 and the octagonal stone **Krishna Temple** was built by a Malla princess after the deaths of both her father and her son, to gain merit for them in their next life.

Leave the Durbar Square by the northwest corner, past some little shops, and find your way down the street to the right to the small entrance guarded by

Inside the 'Golden Temple' or Kwa Bahal

lions of the **Kwa Bahal** or **Golden Temple**, on your left. The most beautifully decorated of all the hundreds of two-storey Newari Buddhist monastery courtyards (for which Patan is renowned), this is an active and busy religious centre. The entire façade of the temple enshrining the Buddha is of finely executed and lavishly embellished gilded copper.

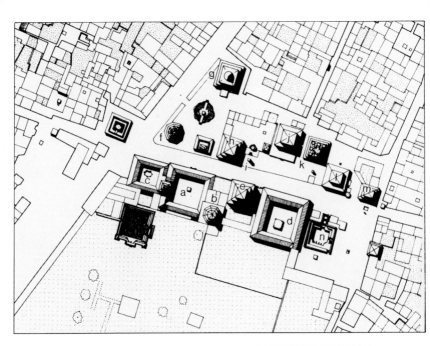

Turn left out of the Kwa Bahal and further north is the towering **Kumbeshwar Temple**. Founded in 1392, it is the oldest in Patan and within its precincts are some early sculptures and two tanks, believed to be fed by waters from the sacred **Gosainkund Lake** high in the **Helambu** mountains. This is where the Hindu Brahmans must renew their sacred threads during the **Janai Purnima** (full moon) festival in July or August. Don't miss the **Ulmanta Bhairav** shrine south of the main temple with its fine silverwork. The northern **Ashoka stupa** is just north of here in this particularly interesting and old corner of Patan. Turning right out of the temple compound follow the road left, the stupa will be visible on the left. Cross the river and you could walk to Baneswar, enjoy

Patan Durbar Square

(a) Mul Chowk and Patan Museum
(b) Taleju Temple
(c) Sundari Chowk
(d) Mani Keshar Chowk
(e) Degutalle
(f) Krishna Temple
(g) Bhai Dega Shiva Temple
(h) Hari Shankar
(i) Siddhi Narasinha Malla
(j) Char Narayan Mandir
(k) Krishna Mandir
(l) Bishwarnath Mandir
(m) Bhimsen Mandir
(n) Mangal Hiti

the view from the top of the **Everest Hotel**, then catch a cab back.

Alternatively, return by a different route turning right to the little **Uma Maheshwar**, with its beautiful 10th-century stone carving of Shiva and Parvati, restored by the Kathmandu Valley Preservation Trust. Passing through the Durbar Square, turn left (east), through the bustle of the vegetable market, down a narrow brick-paved street to the large terrace square containing the **Sundhara** or golden tap. Believed to have been built to refresh the deity **Rato Machhendra**, it is an important stopping place for his chariot. Turn right up a paved street. At the top is the narrow entrance to the remarkable terracotta **Mahabuddha**, or the Temple of the Thousand Buddhas. It was badly damaged in the 1934 earthquake and the restorers, confused by the great many parts that they could not replace, assembled them into another shrine in the corner. Further down the street on the left is the famous **Uku Bahal**, a renowned monastery with gilded roofs and metal animals. Recently restored in a Japanese-funded project, it's one of the earliest *bahals*, built in the 1650s by King Shivadeva.

2. Kirtipur

The ridge city of Kirtipur was the last to fall to the forces of King Prithvi Narayan Shah in 1769.

Cycle or drive through the rather desultory new **Tribhuvan University** buildings and climb up to the ridge-top Newar city of **Kirtipur**. It was the last town to fall to the forces of King Prithvi Narayan Shah during his successful conquest of the Valley in 1768 and 1769: he was apparently so enraged by the resistance and independence of the people of Kirtipur that, when he finally overcame them, he had the noses and lips cut off all the menfolk, sparing only flute players.

Start by visiting the stupa of **Chilanchu Vihar**, which surmounts the southern hill, and step around the piles of grain drying on its stone flags. Once a thriving monastery, this neglected area has four smaller stupas at cardinal points around the central stupa. Wind through the narrow medieval streets, past the ladies spinning in doorways, and the children who will offer you little dolls made from remnants of the local homemade fabric industry. The clunk of the handlooms becomes a familiar sound as you pass the houses

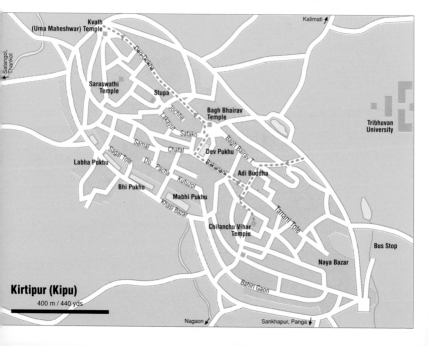

Kirtipur (Kipu)

400 m / 440 yds

of Kirtipur. Walking west, soon you come to a tank in the middle of the town sited below the great **Bagh Bhairav Temple (Mandir)** an imposing building decorated with the daggers, swords and shields captured by King Prithvi Narayan Shah; it is a place of worship for Hindus and Buddhists alike.

The **Kvath** or **Uma Maheshwar Temple (Mandir)** is at the highest point west of the town, guarded by two elephants atop a flight of steps. It commands a fine view across the whole Valley to the distant white Himalaya. Kirtipur has a forgotten feeling about it which makes it rather special, perhaps because of its dramatic and independent history.

3. Pashupatinath and Guhyeshwari

Visit two sacred shrines that Hindus make pilgrimages to.

Pashupatinath (*see map on page 20*) is considered one of the four most important Shiva shrines in Asia and is thus the object of many pilgrimages, especially during festivals such as **Shivaratri**, when tens of thousands of devotees gather here to celebrate Shiva's birthday in February or March.

The largest temple complex in the Kathmandu Valley, it is so sacred that non-Hindus are forbidden to enter its courtyards. There is however still much to see, not least the cremations that are almost constantly being conducted on the banks of the Bagmati, which flows eventually into the holy Ganges. To have their feet in the sacred river at the moment of death is important for Hindus to attain instant release. Two large burning *ghats* directly beneath the main temple are reserved exclusively for members of the royal family. Upstream there are several caves, formerly used by *sadhus* or holy men for meditation, where the river twists into a gorge above the main temple.

The temple is dedicated to Pashupati, the Lord of the Beasts, an incarnation of Shiva particularly popular in Nepal. The present structure was built in 1696 on a 15th-century site by Bupalendra Malla, after the previous building had been severely damaged by termites. Like many Valley temples, the gilded copper triple roofs are decorative, and do not have corresponding floors.

The best approach is from the **Bagmati Bridge** on Ring Road, opposite the modest clubhouse of the Royal Nepal Golf Club. The golf course is on land and is actually owned by the temple *guthi*. Having explored the shrines and sculptures in the environs

Tij festival at Pashupatinath

Shrine at Swayambhunath

of Pashupatinath, cross the two stone bridges, climb up the long flight of steps opposite and pause on the terrace to have a look down on the complex. At the top of the hillock is the **Gorakhnath Shikhara**, and walking on through the forest down the other side, you reach **Guhyeshwari**, the counterpart to Pashupatinath, dedicated to Shiva's *shakti*, Kali. Records of this temple complex, access to which is also forbidden to non-Hindus, date from the 17th century.

4. Swayambhunath and Ichangu

Bijeshwari. Breakfast at the Hotel Vajra, then up to the all-seeing eyes of Swayambhunath, the oldest settlement in the Valley. Finish the morning with a walk to the village shrine of Ichangu Narayan.

If you are in a car, you might like to include a visit to the **National Museum** in **Chauni** (open 9am to 4pm, closed Tuesdays) to admire its collection of sculptures and scroll paintings. The best direct approach to **Bijeshwari** is on foot from Kathmandu, about half an hour walk, crossing the river over the **Vishnumati Bridge**. Instead of following the road left, climb the steps ahead of you to the **Bijeshwari Temple**. This Tantric shrine is especially interesting in the early morning when local people gather with their daily offerings. Stop for breakfast (or lunch) on the roof of the **Hotel**

Vajra, situated just above the river, and enjoy the view of both the Swayambhunath Hill and over the city from this remarkable hotel. Don't miss the painted ceiling in the Great Pagoda Room at the very top of the building.

The magnificent setting of **Swayambhunath Stupa** dominates this area as you approach it by the tarmac road. Climb the pilgrim's route up the 365 stone steps on the eastern side of the forested hill, flanked with the great animal vehicles of the five Dhyani-Buddhas (meditating buddhas) – Amogasiddhi on Garuda (north), Akshobhya on elephant (east), Patmasambhava on horse (south), Amitabha on peacock (west) and Vairocana on lion (near Akshobhya). The Dhyani-Buddhas represent the qualities attached to a Boddhisattva (Enlightened One).

Between the Buddhas we find four Buddhashakis which represent the female qualities. All around the stupa you see prayer mills with the prayer inscription '*Om mani padme hum*'. Spinning around the prayer mill (always clockwise like the surrounding stupa) saves the believers saying the prayer. Bunches of monkeys in the whole area gave the stupa its nickname Monkey Temple. Make sure you don't hold any sort of food in your hands while strolling around here, as the monkeys are known for becoming quite aggressive in order to grab a snack. A huge gilded copper *vajra* (Tibetan: *dorje*), or thunderbolt, a symbol of absolute power, awaits you at the top.

The all-seeing eyes of supreme Buddhahood gaze from beneath the great gilded pinnacle with its 13 rings and crowning parasol. The nose, which looks rather like an incomplete question mark, is the Nepalese number 'one', *ek*, a symbol of unity.

The stupa is also surrounded by a great number of buildings, shrines and a little Tibetan monastery which you are most welcome to visit. Four of the shrines are dedicated to the four elements: earth, water, fire and air. Another one on the northeast side of the Stupa is dedicated to Hariti (also known as Ajima), the goddess of smallpox. Mothers would come here with their children to let the goddess immunise them against smallpox and other diseases.

On the northern end is the rather inconspicuous Shantipur Building. It has a very interesting story: after King Gunakamadeva made the gods angry due to inbreeding, a terrible drought and famine came over the land. With the help of a wise man called Shantikar, who lived in the building, the king tried to calm down the elements. Shantikar succeeded in gaining rule over nine *nags* (gods of snakes). He made them pay homage to the king and out of their own blood they built their images – afterwards rain was supposed to fall. Even nowadays it is said that the king of Nepal comes to the temple once in a while praising the nine snake gods.

Mingle with monks, devout Nepalis and Tibetan pilgrims prostrating themselves full-length in reverence around the stupa that is the ancient lotus island of Manjushri's Valley lake. There is little doubt that this site was established more than 2,500 years ago. Having browsed among the shrines, sculptures and monasteries, (avoiding the monkeys) and admired the incomparable view of the valley, leave by the west side of the hill, picking up the car at the parking place by the monastery halfway up.

Head on down the hill and through the village to Ring Road, here bordered by a wall of prayer wheels and street sellers, and strung across with fluttering prayer flags. Cross the highway and take the road west, directly opposite the road you've just come down. The car, if you have one, must wait where the road peters out at a little shrine on a steep saddle. From here it is a half-hour walk partly through rice and mustard fields, cacti and stone quarries to **Ichangu Narayan**, a temple on the south side of **Nagarjun Hill**.

The two-storey temple was founded, according to legend, by King Hari Datta in the 6th century but the present building is 18th century. It is one of the four important Narayan shrines that, after a period of fasting, must be visited in one day in the **Haribodhini Ekadasi** in October or November when Vishu is welcomed back from his long summer sleep. The other three are Bishankhu Narayan, Changu Narayan and Sekh Narayan.

Hindu cremation

5. Bagmati Ghats

Explore the Bagmati ghats and temples of Pachali Bhairav, Tindeval, Tripura Sundari and Hem Narayan (Kalamochan). Easily reached, this seldom-visited area reveals an intimate glimpse of daily life. However, this area is now very run-down and pollution in the river and on the banks is a serious problem.

Start walking from **Tripureswar** at the small shrine of **Nav Durga** opposite the modest little Valley View Hotel. From here a dirt road leads to the holy **Bagmati River** and to the temple of the **Pachali Bhairav**, nestled in a tabernacle within the roots of a *pipal* tree. This shrine, to one of the most venerated forms of Shiva, is guarded by the sleeping **Baital**, who is worshipped on Tuesday and Saturday evenings, adorned with flowers and rice, and smeared with vermilion powder.

Walk on to the river, past the crumbling **Laxmeswar Shrine** on the right, where most of the courtyard has gone and much of the woodcarving is going. The charm of this area lies in its living decay. Across the footbridge are the mineral springs of the **Rajghat**.

Turn left along the Bagmati *ghats* where Hindus traditionally burn their dead, though today a cremation is more likely to be further west at **Tekuo** at the confluence of the Vishnumati with the Bagmati rivers. Behind the *chaityas* and statues is the interesting temple complex of **Tindeval**, a fine example of the Indian *shikhara* style. Nepal's religious harmony is visible in Shiva's trident standing next to Buddhist symbols of enlightenment. Walk 10 minutes down the path along the riverbank, past the pottery that makes decorative balustrades, and past the brick and stucco police barracks, until the roofs of the **Tripura Sundari** can be seen set back to the left within a fine courtyard. Built in 1818 by Queen Tripurasundari, the temple stands on a broad base with small temples at each corner and roof struts depicting stories from the *Mahabharata* epic.

The splendid white dome of the **Hem Narayan** or **Kalamochan**, guarded by rampant golden lions at each corner, is a little further on past a handsome red-smeared Hanuman, the monkey god, and across a small stream. This temple of obvious Moghul influence was built in 1852 by Jung Bahadur Rana to celebrate victories at war. It has a very fine statue of him set on a stone pillar and good woodcarvings. Leave the Hem Narayan by the opposite gate from the river and you are back in Tripureswar, close to **Patan Bridge**.

6. The Great Ashoka Stupas

Visit the four historically evocative stupas (the fifth central one is lost) which, if indeed erected in the 3rd century BC by Emperor Ashoka, the Mauryan king of northern India, make Patan the oldest Buddhist city in the world.

You will need a car or taxi for this unusual circuit of ancient stupas. Except for the eastern one which is plastered and whitewashed, the typical shallow domes of the stupas remain grass-covered.

Life on the street: a Tamang woman washes her reluctant son

47

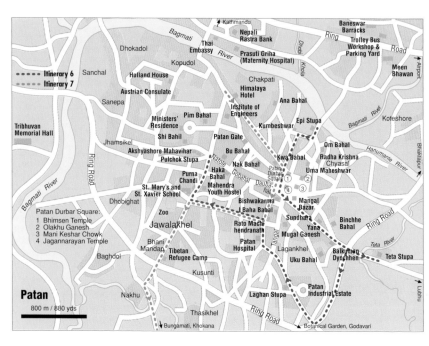

Start with the northern **Epi Stupa** behind the **Kumbeshwar Temple** to which it is best to walk from the Patan Durbar Square (*see Itinerary 1, Pick & Mix*). Returning to the Durbar Square, drive east through the winding narrow streets of the eastern outskirts of Patan to Ring Road. Straight across, the eastern **Teta Stupa** (my favourite) stands forgotten amidst fields on the left of the little-used road to **Lubhu**.

Follow Ring Road south; instead of taking the route left at the crossroads to **Godavari**, turn right. After a short distance is the southern **Lagan Stupa**. The top is supposed to be the only point in the Valley from where you can see Mount Everest. Go on down the road. You pass on the right the extensive buildings of the Patan Hospital and on your left the outskirts of Patan.

To reach the fourth western stupa, turn right at the zoo round-about at **Jawalakhel**; look out for the Hotel Narayani as you go down the hill and the **Pulchowk Stupa** is opposite on the left. Explore behind it and climb to the restored **Akshyashore Mahavihar** on an early Licchavi site.

7. Follow the Rato Machhendra

See the boutiques of Baber Mahal Revisited, have an early lunch at Chez Caroline or one of the other restaurants here, then visit Patan, Jawalakhel and the 16th-century country villages of Khokana and Bungamati, winter home of the Rato Machhendra.

After breakfast at your hotel take a taxi to **Baber Mahal**, where

part of this old Rana palace has been converted into 40 chic boutiques and restaurants. Although the shops are expensive, the seven courtyards are well worth seeing. Have lunch at **Chez Caroline** (tel: 01-263070) and pick up your taxi again to continue to Patan. Leaving the taxi, skirt the Durbar Square and head south to one of the most popular temples in Patan, the **Rato Machhendranath Temple**, dedicated to the powerful Tantric deity who guards the Valley and is worshipped as the god of rain and plenty. His beautiful temple stands in an open square and has intricately carved doorways and struts, and graceful windbells lining the metal roofs.

The **Rato Machhendra** is paraded through Patan every summer in a huge chariot culminating in the festival of **Bhoto Jatra** at **Jawalakhel**. The exact month is fixed by astrologers, and a sacred bejewelled waistcoat, or *bhoto*, supposedly belonging to the serpent king, is displayed in the presence of the royal family. The chariot is then dismantled, except once every 12 years (the next occasion is in 2003) when the chariot is dragged to the Rato Machhendra's second residence at **Bungamati**, a village 5km (3 miles) south down a steep and rugged road. This is a difficult task undertaken very seriously because, it is said, if the chariot fails to reach Bungamati within a certain time, the god will be taken to Bhaktapur.

You may wish to visit the **Patan Zoo** with its man-eating tiger brought from Chitwan. It is said that the Patan Zoo is in itself a museum of sad Victorian zoo conditions. Explore the good Tibetan carpet shops around the **Tibetan Refugee Camp** and call in to watch them being dyed and woven in the traditional manner. Handmade carpets are Nepal's biggest export industry.

Take a taxi or have your car meet you here and, crossing Ring Road, take the processionary route, lined with votive *chaityas*, to the twin settlements of **Bungamati** and **Khokana**. Visit the *shikara*-style **Rato Machhendranath Temple**, where the powerful deity has spent his winter months since 1593, carried here most years from Patan in a simple palanquin except for the marathon when the huge chariot must negotiate this road. Visit the image of Bhairav in his nearby **Lokeswar Shrine**.

From Bungamati it is a short walk to **Khokana**, but be sure to detour uphill to the important Ganesh shrine of **Karya Binayak** set in a pretty forest clearing. The single-storey temple in a walled compound is often busy with families seeking help from the elephant god, Ganesh, who specialises in completing difficult tasks.

There is a beautiful view from this peaceful rural shrine across the yellow mustard fields to the western foothills but, as everywhere in Kathmandu, the area is becoming more developed. When you reach Khokana, seek out the mustard oil presses for which this village is famous for and the **Shekali Mai** shrine, dedicated to one of the Valley's nature goddesses.

8. Manjushri's Gorge and Kali's Sacrifice

Excursion to Chobar, Pharping and Dakshinkali, by car or bicycle, visiting the temples in this historic corner of the Valley.

If you are planning to cycle, take a packed lunch as Dakshinkali, the furthest point, is 22km (14 miles) from Kathmandu.

Stop first at **Chobar** *(see map on page 20)* where, legend tells us, the god Manjushri released the Valley lake by smiting a gorge with his sword. The Bagmati River indeed drains the Valley through a narrow gorge which slices through the Chobar Hill, though today this natural wonder is much disfigured by a belching cement factory. It is hard to ignore the results of its pollution as you climb up the steps to the **Adinath Temple**, a triple-roofed Buddhist temple built in 1640 and decorated with numerous household implements; water vessels, cooking pots and pans. A metal suspension bridge spans the gorge, imported from Scotland in 1903.

Just south is the riverside shrine of **Jal Binayak**, honouring a massive rock **Ganesh**, where people who seek strength of character worship. Also enshrined here is the thunderbolt said to have been hurled at the Valley wall by Krishna in the alternative version of the legend of the lake. The road south passes the small **Taudaha Lake**, created by Manjushri, according to legend, to house the *nagas* (serpents) stranded when the Valley was drained.

Follow the twists and turns of the river, with the bulk of **Champa Devi Hill** (2,279m/7,477ft) looming on the right and take a detour for breakfast or lunch to the **Haatiban Himalayan Heights Resort** (tel: 01-371537) at **Haatiban**. The turning to the right is marked on the telephone pole and the road climbs steeply for 15 minutes to this pleasant hotel on a high flank overlooking the Valley and

Chobar Gorge

white peaks. The main road eventually reaches the lovely town of **Pharping**, just outside the Valley at an altitude of 1,570m (5,148ft). The rock temple of **Sekh Narayan Temple** honours Vishnu and stands above a series of pools full of fish, a place of pilgrimage since the 15th century. Further up the same hill is the thriving Tibetan Buddhist monastery and meditation centre at the **Astura Cave**, sacred to the Tibetan saint, Guru Padma Sambhava, whose supposed footprints, carved on the platform, are dated 1390. Above Pharping is the 17th-century temple of **Bajra Jogini Temple**, not be confused with the Sankhu temple of the same name. The Tantric goddess' pleasant visage belies her awesome instruments, a chopper with a *vajra* handle and skull cap.

Several miles below Pharping is the shrine of **Dakshinkali**, or southern Kali, at the bottom of a flight of stairs in a dark natural recess at a confluence between two forested hillsides. The goddess' insatiable appetite is appeased

Pilgrim at Dakshinkali

by twice-weekly sacrifices, Saturday and Tuesday, when the blood of male goats and chickens bathe the black stone image of Kali, the consort of Shiva in her most terrible form. The headless carcases are transformed into picnics for the faithful on the slopes above this sinister spot. The simpler shrine of Kali's mother is up a hill beyond the lower temple.

9. Bishankhu Narayan

Walk from the Godavari road to the temple of Bishankhu Narayan. Beware, as only those pure of sin can fit through a narrow cleft in the rock. Visit the Royal Botanical Gardens at Godavari.

Leave early in the morning to enjoy the view of the mountains, the activity in the fields and the village life through which you pass. Carry a packed meal to avoid going back early for lunch.

Taking the radial to **Godavari** from Ring Road, pass through the villages of **Harisiddhi Bhawani Temple** and **Thaiba**, reminiscent of a Bruegel masterpiece in their symphony of colours and textures. At the end of the next town, **Baregaon**, take the dirt road northeast. Leave the car at the first village road to await your return and enjoy walking through this magical corner of the Valley.

The road climbs to a saddle from which, on a clear morning, you can see as far west at the white peaks of the **Annapurna** range, north of Pokhara. The temple of **Bishankhu Narayan** is little more than a natural cave at the top of a steep stairway, but it is one of the most celebrated Vishnu shrines in the Valley. According to legend, Shiva once hid here from the demon, Bhasmasur, who had the power to turn all living things into dust and ashes at his touch. Vishnu convinced the demon to touch his own forehead and the demon turned himself to dust; the hillock adjacent to the cave is said to be made of the ashes of Bhasmasur.

After returning to the car, drive on to the village of **Godavari** where the marble quarry scars a hillside on the right. Above you is the highest hill on the rim of the Valley, **Phulchoki** (2,762m/ 9,062ft), which is a lovely place for early morning bird watching and spring walks in the rhododendron forests.

The first boarding school in Nepal was opened in Godavari in 1951 by American Jesuits, who still run one of the finest schools in the Valley. Founded by the late Father Moran – the ham radio enthusiast who was one of the first foreigners to be granted Nepali citizenship – the school welcomes interested educators as visitors.

Pass beneath the tall trees and you will see the stone buildings of the school set back on your right. Follow the road down the hill to the **Royal Botanical Gardens**, well worth a visit and a good place to linger, except on Saturday when its peace is shattered by the mandatory stereos that accompany every party of picnickers.

10. Everest Flight

Mountain flights along the Himalaya to Mount Everest. Your memories of this exhilarating ride will last you a lifetime.

Every morning several of Nepal's airlines have flights east from Kathmandu for one hour along the snow white peaks of the Himalaya

Mount Everest

Kangchenjunga from the air

to view **Mount Everest** (8,848m/29,028ft). The highest mountain in the world sits astride the Nepal-Tibet border, and is known as Sagarmatha (Mother of the Universe) in Nepal and as Chomolungma (Mother Goddess of the Snow) in Tibet. Lifting even the most jaded of spirits, this flight to enchantment is an opportunity to enjoy the subtle colours of the intricate cobweb of terraced hillsides of the Mahabharat, or middle hills, as well as to glory in the awesome heights and ranges of the highest chain of mountains in the world.

Most local airlines operate flights. **Buddha Air** (tel: 01-4188 64) is recommended for its new fleet of speedy Beech 16-seaters.

Nepal, Top Of The World

A mecca for mountaineers, climbers and trekkers, Nepal has eight of the 10 highest mountains in the world and eight of the world's fourteen 8,000m (26,250ft) peaks within or on its borders. They are:

1.	**Everest** (Sagarmatha, Chomolungma) in the Himalaya range on Nepal-Tibet (China) border	8,850m 29,028ft
2.	**K-2** (Chogari; sometimes called Mt. Goodwin Austin, but this name is not officially recognised) in the Karakorum range on the Pakistan-China border	8,611m 28,251ft
3.	**Kangchenjunga** Himalaya, Nepal-India border	8,586m 28,169ft
4.	**Lhotse** Himalaya, Nepal-Tibet border	8,516m 27,940ft
5.	**Makalu** Himalaya, Nepal-Tibet border	8,463m 27,766ft
6.	**Cho Oyu** Himalaya, Nepal-Tibet border	8,201m 26,906ft
7.	**Dhaulagiri 1** Himalaya, Nepal	8,167m 26,795ft
8.	**Manaslu** Himalaya, Nepal	8,163m 26,781ft
9.	**Nanga Parbat** Hindu Kush, Pakistan	8,125m 26,657ft
10.	**Annapurna 1** Himalaya, Nepal	8,091m 26,545ft
11.	**Gasherbrum 1** Karakoram, Pakistan (Hidden Peak)	8,068m 26,470ft
12.	**Broad Peak** Karakoram, Pakistan	8,047m 26,401ft
13.	**Shisha Pangma** (Xixabangma, Gosainthan) Himalaya, Tibet (China)	8,046m 26,398ft
14.	**Gasherbrum 11** Karakoram, Pakistan	8,035m 26,362ft

Day TRIPS

11. Sankhu Goddess and Gokarna Golf Course

Explore the old trading town of Sankhu and the shrine of the Bajra Jogini. Return for lunch and in the afternoon, enjoy the facilities at the Gokarna Forest Reserve.

Arrange a car for the day or taxi the 19km (12 miles) to the town of **Sankhu** *(see map on page 20)*, in the northeast part of the Valley, a historical stop on the old trading route to Tibet. After investigating the town, follow the road that continues only a little way north beyond the town and becomes a wide path, paved with stone. The important temple to the mysterious goddess **Bajra Jogini** is a climb up a steep flight of steps hidden among tall dark pines. She is portrayed in a fine gold

Spotted deer or chital

torana above the door of the three-roofed structure; notice the roof struts with figures of various deities. The neighbouring **Gunivihar Temple** has an interesting *chaitya*. There are other shrines and sculptures in the **Vajra Yogini Dyochhen**, further up the hill. Legend has the Tantric goddess residing here from primeval history, and she is credited with having persuaded Manjushri to drain the Valley lake.

Rejoin your car in Sankhu and return down the road to the **Gokarna Forest Reserve,** also known as **Gokarna Safari Park**, where you can take an elephant ride to see wildlife such as *chital*, or monkeys. Bird watching is also good here, particularly in the late afternoon and early morning. To the north of the park is the ancient pagoda-style temple of **Gokarna Mahadev**, renovated by King Jayasthiti Malla in 1422 *(See page 30)*.

Do a round of prayer wheels at **Bodhnath**, which you will pass on the way back. Remember, it is most auspicious to circumambulate an odd number of times, and always clockwise, keeping the stupa on your right.

12. Tantric Temple and Shiva Screen at Lele

A bicycle ride (or arrange a car for the day) through the southern Valley towns of Sunakothi, Thecho, Chapagaon and Lele visiting the temples of Vajra Varahi and Tika Bhairav.

Turn off Ring Road and head south at the turning marked with a red sign to the Leprosy Hospital at Anandaban, just west of the Godavari turning – be careful as some local maps are misleading. This will be an enchanting rural day in a little-known corner south of the Valley. You will enjoy the terraced green rice fields, scarlet poinsettias and spikey brown cactus in the hedgerows, with always the chance of wide views of the white mountains behind.

The road passes through the 16th-century town of **Sunakothi** *(see map on page 20)* but you might be tempted to stop a while in the next, more friendly, settlement of **Thecho**. The **Balkumari Temple** overlooks a square used for drying golden grain and red chillies, and plenty of noisy clamouring children.

A mile (1.6km) on is the old town of **Chapagaon** still pleasant despite the building development in the area. There are some erotic carvings on the **Bhairav Shrine** in the village. Follow the path east out of the town to the important Tantric site of the **Vajra Varahi Temple**, in a grove of sacred trees. Naturally shaped stones are worshipped here as images of Ganesh, Bhairav and the Ashta Matrikas and on the edge of the trees are some old cremation grounds.

Returning to the main road south, there is a particularly good place to eat your picnic lunch, with fine views and shady trees, if you can find it. The spot is tucked high above the left side of the road on a corner just before it drops down into the **Lele Valley**. Visit the eye-opening **Leprosy Hospital** in the village of **Anandaban**, which is well marked with red and white signs.

Chapagaon from the Lele road

If you have the energy to continue on down the deteriorating road, be sure to look for the **Tika Bhairav** shrine to the right of the road on the edge of the village of **Lele**. It is not a temple in any conventional sense. Look for a huge brick wall, 2 by 6m (10 by 20ft) painted with a wonderful, monumental abstract close-up of Bhairav, Shiva in his most terrible form. Lele is just beyond the edge of the Valley and the drive to this remote corner is well rewarded with unspoiled countryside and clean fresh air.

13. Sleeping Vishnus and Kakani Emissaries

Balaju Vishnu and the 22 Water Spouts. Drive to Kakani. Walk to Budhanilkantha and see the sleeping Vishnu before returning.

Arrange a car and driver for the day and start by visiting the Licchavi **Balaju Reclining Vishnu** and the **22 Water Spouts**, the largest *hiti* in the Kathmandu Valley and always crowded with people washing and bathing. These are located *(see map on page 20)* in the small park on the left in the town of **Balaju** just across Ring Road, northwest of Kathmandu. At the foot of the forested **Nagarjun hill**, the park is a popular place for bird watchers and picnickers, with a special corner always thronging with locals. Try to avoid the public swimming pool.

Drive on past the main entrance to the Nagarjun forest and wind up the Trisuli road for about one hour (29km/18 miles) through the terraces and bamboo stands. At the very top, turn sharp right to **Kakani**, a small village perched high on the rim of the Valley.

Kakani has a large police training school and a wonderful view. Enjoy it from the garden of the **Taragaon Hotel** and peek over the barbed-wire fence at the original Raj-style bungalow that has belonged to successive British emissaries since 1850.

Britain's close links with Nepal date back to the early 19th century when the armies of the Nepalese Shah dynasty were pushing back the borders of the country into what the British East India Company believed to be their territory. In 1814 the two countries went to war and it was as part of the Treaty of Segauli, signed with Britain in 1816, that Nepal was forced to accept a permanent British ambassador, or Resident, as he was known.

At that time the British Resident's movements were greatly restricted, even within the Valley which he was forbidden to leave, and this property was given by Jung Bahadur Rana himself as their own private retreat. Carried up by servants or arriving on ponies with their own personal army bodyguards, here the first foreign residents of Nepal could relax uninhibited by the restrictions and formalities of 19th-century court life. They were free to play golf or hunt for barking deer, *chukor* partridge or pheasant, signalling when in need of further supplies to their Kathmandu Residence by heliograph, a complicated system of flashing mirrors which relied on line of sight.

Reclining Vishnu at Budhanilkantha

Leave the car, and be sure the driver knows you wish to be met beside the great Vishnu at Budhanilkantha. Set off northeast along the line of the ridge towards the fruit farm, then seek local advice to find the road that bears east around the flanks of the **Shivapuri Hills** – the highest peak is 2,732m (8,940ft).

Resist the temptation to go down to your right or you will end up back in Balaju. It can be warm on this south-facing hill so be sure you carry adequate drinking water. Continue for about four hours, picnicking on the way, and enjoy the wonderful view south over the entire Kathmandu Valley.

Eventually you will reach the village of **Budhanilkantha** which is close to the vanished Licchavi town called Thatungri Dranga. Pass the brick-built compound of the British-subsidised secondary school, where the Crown Prince was a former pupil, and visit the ancient **Reclining Vishnu**.

The largest and most powerful of the four Vishnus in the Valley, this massive Licchavi sculpture of the Reclining Vishnu is made from a massive black stone that must have been dragged from far beyond the Valley. Lying on a bed of huge coiled *nagas* or serpents, a forecast of death forbids the kings of Nepal, themselves incarnations of Vishnu, from looking at the monumental image. Renovations have sadly felled the *pipal* tree which shaded the image and imprisoned it behind concrete bars. From here it is only a 9-km (6-mile) drive south to Kathmandu.

14. Dhulikhel to Panauti

Long day hike from Dhulikhel, via Namo Buddha, to Panauti.

This is a good five-hour walk and nearly two hours' drive in total, so leave Kathmandu latest by 8.30am after breakfast. Carry a daypack with a waterbottle and a packed lunch. You will need a taxi to drop you at **Dhulikhel** *(see map on page 20)*. Ask the driver to pick you up at about 3pm from Panauti and ask him to wait by the Brahmayani Temple at the confluence of the rivers.

Turn right into the town of Dhulikhel, then left past the new buildings and government offices in this regional headquarters. Start walking up a wide well-worn trail and soon the climb reaches a little shrine and you are rewarded by spectacular mountain views extending as far west as the **Annapurnas** and even **Dhaulagiri** on a good day. Asking people as you go and skirting the jeep track, it will take you about three hours to reach the gleaming white stupa of **Namo Buddha** on the **Namara hill**. It is a lovely, varied walk through fields and forests with constantly delightful views and, at one point, a rather alarming landslide. Explore the prayer-flag-bedecked stupa, monasteries and *mani* walls. Important to Tibetan Buddhists, this sacred spot is where, according to legend, the Lord Buddha offered himself to a starving tigress and her cubs.

Eat lunch with a 360° view on the very highest point before dropping down on the western side of the hill to **Namara**, with its Swayambhunath-like stupa and huge prayer wheel. The trail descends steeply through sacred forests, then meanders through villages and cultivated fields along a pretty valley. Take note of some remarkable Ganesh shrines and fine woodcarvings on the *dharmasalas*, or travellers' resthouses, in the villages on this pilgrims' route. This is the most impressive approach to **Panauti**, and the artistic jumble of temple roofs clustered at the **confluence** of the Pungamati and Roshi rivers gleam in the sun. Be sure to find the energy to explore this fascinating town *(see Day 2 itinerary)* with its very early and precious temples.

Right, pilgrim route to Namo Buddha

EXCURSIONS

Despite the density of the richness of Kathmandu Valley, the real wealth of Nepal can only be appreciated by a visit to the mountains, rivers and jungles beyond the Valley. Nepal is compact, so the diversity intrinsic in this beautiful country can be enjoyed in a series of well-planned overnight visits.

Nepal is criss-crossed with trails and trade routes, making it ideal for trekking trips of four days to four weeks or more. Trekking requires not only time, but an enjoyment of camping and walking, as there are inevitable ups and downs in the Himalayan terrain, and flat ridge walking is relatively rare. With a reputable agent, trekking is a luxurious experience compared with the Westerner's concept of backpacking. Not only are there porters to carry all but a light daypack, but tents are erected, tables and stools provided and meals cooked by an unfailingly cheerful team of Sherpa guides.

Nepal's road network is less comprehensive, so without the time or desire to trek, these suggestions are necessarily restricted to driving and flying. The routes that follow will give you a feel of Nepal. Combine them as you please; link them into a longer trip, or choose one if your time is short.

Rhododendrons, with Machhapuchhre's distinctive Fishtail peak

15. Trisuli River

Drive early down the Pokhara road to the Trisuli River. Spend the day river running in rubber rafts, riding the rapids and enjoying the scenery at the leisurely speed of the river. Camp overnight on a white-sand beach. Next day, continue down river, then drive back to Kathmandu.

Several huge river systems drain the Himalaya, tumbling from the heights of Tibet fed by milky glaciers, racing past the terraces of the middle hills until they slow down, passing through the **Terai** lowlands and meandering into the Ganges. The middle stretches of these rivers with evocative names such as the **Bheri**, the **Karnali**, the **Kali Gandaki**, the **Seti**, the **Sunkoshi**, the **Dudh Kosi** and the **Arun** can take days and even weeks to run.

With the advantage of both convenience and accessibility, a two-day trip on the **Trisuli River** offers a lovely opportunity to experience the joys of rural Nepal at the relaxed pace of the river. Choose a reliable operator, and they will make all the arrangements at a fixed cost. This will include securing a river permit, arranging the car, providing the boat and a trained crew, all meals and all camping equipment. **Himalayan River Exploration** (tel: 01-411225) and **Ultimate Descents** (tel: 01-439526) are two professionally-run rafting companies that maintain stringent safety standards and offer the best facilities.

The road climbs out of the early-morning Valley past the town of **Thankot**, the earth-satellite station and King Tribhuvan's polite wave. With clear skies, the first glimpse of **Himalchuli** (7,893m/25,896ft) and **Manaslu** (8,163m/26,781ft), will take your breath away as you reach the rim. The main road to India drops down to the truck-stop village of **Naubise**, where it divides. Branch right and on through the hills until you get to the put-in point at the village of **Kuringhat**, where you bump down to the river edge over sculptured stones and crashing waters. Your personal belongings are stowed in black waterproof bags and sealed ammunition boxes.

Although always within reach of the road, the river trip travels self-sufficient of camping gear, food, drink, first-aid kit and helpers to assist in both rowing and camping, as well as interpreting the sights and sounds of the riverside villages and the flora and fauna of the riverbanks.

Pausing at a wayside shrine, exploring a simple settlement or waving at curious children, a day on the river is hard to beat. Between the adrenalin rush of the rapids, all with alluring names and some of which change with the seasons, the flat, calm stretches provide ample opportunity for swimming, relaxing and simply reflecting. Sleep in tents on the sand beaches after an evening around a driftwood fire.

The river trip ends early afternoon of the second day, when the imposing bridge at the roadside town of **Mugling** comes into view. Here the road divides to **Pokhara** (a three-hour drive) or to **Narayanghat** (one hour). It is about three hours' drive back to Kathmandu. If there is time, another day floating on the river brings you to the **Royal Chitwan National Park** *(see Itinerary 17, Excursions)*, a beautiful wildlife park.

For more information on white water rafting in Nepal consult Knowles' & Allardice's *White Water Nepal*, available in bookshops in Kathmandu.

Machhapuchhre and the Annapurnas reflected in Phewa Lake, Pokhara

16. Pokhara: Magnificent Mountains

The verdant Pokhara valley is 200km (124 miles) west of Kathmandu. The old trading bazaar of Pokhara, beneath the towering Annapurna Himal, is dominated by the distinctive peak of Machhapuchhre, the sacred Fishtail. Stay for one or two nights by the lakeside to enjoy the sleepy atmosphere and superb views.

Take a half-hour flight from Kathmandu west to **Pokhara** along the mountains, sitting on the right side of the aircraft for the best view. Driving takes six hours, and longer if you detour to the restored 15th-century palace and temple of **Gorkha**, seat of King Prithvi Narayan Shah, who united Nepal in 1768 and founded the present dynasty. Ideally, drive there from Kathmandu, and fly back.

Set in the wide, lush, green valley of the **Seti River**, the old trading town of Pokhara sprawls over several miles. Decorated pony trains from the Kali Gandaki trade routes jostle with men from the mountains bartering in the bazaar. Buses hoot and trekkers stride down the street *en route* for the hills.

More peaceful is the **Phewa Lake**, south of the airstrip and the main town. On a clear morning the snowy outlines of the **Annapurna Himal** and the **Fishtail** peak of **Machhapuchhre** are reflected in its depths. Enjoy the restful atmosphere of this almost tropical valley of Nepal. Jacaranda, banana and papaya trees flourish at this altitude of about 900m (3,000ft).

Boats are available on the lake; you can row yourself or be rowed. Tourists visit the **Mahendra Caves** and the **Hyangja Tibetan Village** but more fun is the **Tibetan Camp** at **Pardi** and **Devi's Fall** (also Patale Chhango), where the river disappears underground into a sinister hole (entrance fees).

If you want to do more than relax, there are numerous day hikes in the hills around Pokhara. You can walk up to the viewpoint at **Sarangkot** in two to three hours from Binde Basini Temple in the town centre but it's uphill almost all the way. **Laxmi Lodge** (tel: 061-21523, email: oskar@mos.com.np), in the village of **Birethanti**, is an upmarket trekking lodge that makes an even more convenient base than Pokhara for short walks. Staffed by Gurkhas, it's just a 20-minute walk from Nayapul and the main road to Pokhara (40km/25 miles).

Sixteen kilometres (10 miles) east of Pokhara is **Begnas Tal**, a lake in a peaceful location. **Tiger Mountain Pokhara Lodge** (tel: 01-411225, email: info@tigermountain.com) is a luxury mountain resort that has just opened here in a picturesque spot with superb views.

In and around Pokhara there are almost 200 guesthouses and hotels to suit every budget. If you want to be right in the centre of the busy tourist area by the lake, the **Hotel the Hungry Eye** (tel: 061-20908) offers clean budget accommodation Several new up-market hotels have opened recently in Pokhara. The most comfort-able are the **Shangri-La Village Pokhara** (tel: 061-22122, email: hosangp@village.mos.com.np) and the **Fulbari Resort** (tel: 061-23451, email: resv@fulbari.com.np); both have swimming pools and superb mountain views.

17. Chitwan Jungle Jaunt

In one of the most beautiful wildlife areas in Asia, Tiger Tops has been operating memorable trips to this former hunting re-serve well before it became Royal Chitwan National Park. Choose from a combination of nights at the world-famous Tiger Tops Jungle Lodge, the Tented Camp for wildlife devotees or the Tharu Village for a taste of village life on the edge of the jungle.

It is a half-hour flight (every day) to Tiger Tops' **Meghauli** grass airstrip, where you are met and escorted by landrover or elephant across the **Buri Rapti River** and into **Royal Chitwan National Park** (900 sq km/350 sq miles). This airstrip was extended at the visit of Queen Elizabeth II in 1961 for what was to be one of the last of the great tiger hunts in this historic region, where royalty and viceroys had been hosted for decades by the rulers of Nepal. Tiger Tops can also be reached by a five-hour drive from Kathmandu or Pokhara, or a three-day trip down the river.

The survival of the **Terai** wildlife of Nepal was threatened when

Tiger Tops safari tents

the endemic malaria was eradicated in the 1950s, and large num-bers of hill people began to settle in the Chitwan valley, clear-ing the forest habitat for cultivation. Chit-wan is at an altitude of 140m (450ft): the fear of an unknown Nepal, and malaria fever had effectively acted as a southern blockade be-fore, deterring potential invaders and isolating the few indigenous

Viewing Greater One-horned rhinoceros

Tharu people who had developed a partial resistance to the disease.

Opened in 1973, this park was first set aside to protect not the magnificent **Royal Bengal tiger**, but the **Greater One-horned rhinoceros** whose prehistoric bulk, with its characteristic folds of skin, thrives in the tall grassland areas of the lowland **Terai**. The animal was once hunted for its lucrative horn valued by the Chinese for medicinal properties, but poaching is now virtually unknown. Another important endangered species found in the Narayani River is the **Gharial crocodile**, with its long narrow snout developed for catching fish. The wildlife of Chitwan is rich and diverse, with over 450 species of birds, including all the summer migrants and winter visitors.

The elephant grass grows to 8m (25ft) in height and makes the domestic elephant an essential and practical means of conveyance. Some species of the mixed riverine forest include the *bombax*, or silk cotton tree, with its red blossom and later, white cotton which showers the forest floor, and the brilliant orange flame-of-the-forest. The tall *sal* trees (*Shorea robusta*), with their large, flat leaves grow on higher ground in the **Siwalik (Churia) Range**, the last wave of the Himalaya along the Indian border. This part of the park is home to the elusive **gaur**, the world's largest wild cattle.

Tiger Tops (PO Box 242, Kathmandu, tel: 01-411225, fax: 414075, email: info@tigermountain.com) will show you the glories of Chitwan, from the elegant tree-top rooms of **Tiger Tops Jungle Lodge** in the heart of the park, or from the comfort of the **Tented Camp** on a plateau commanding views across the whole width of Nepal. There are knowledgeable naturalists, guide

Machans, or blinds, for wildlife viewing

65

walks and landrover-drives through the forest, visits to *machans* (hides) overlooking *tals* (small lakes) and boat trips down the Rapti and Narayani rivers. The best part is riding the elephants in search of wild animals, or bathing with them in the river at the elephant camp.

First opened in 1964, Tiger Tops pioneered controlled eco-sensitive tourism with its solar energy, wildlife research programmes and educational services for the local communities.

The **Tiger Tops Tharu Village**, set in a beautiful wild garden on the edge of the park, offers a combination of more general wildlife and cultural activities and is open all the year round. The spacious rooms are styled after Tharu longhouses, decorated with artefacts and mud paintings; there is a swimming pool, tennis court, nightly local dancing and a stable of horses and ponies on which to explore the surrounding countryside and villages.

18. Karnali Wildlife Wonders

Royal Bardia National Park, in far west Nepal, is the favoured destination for the true wilderness enthusiast, rich in all the wildlife of the subcontinent. The two-hour drive from Nepalganj to Tiger Tops Karnali Lodge and Tented Camp is through virgin forest and attractive Tharu villages.

Providing you have at least three nights and a real interest in wild places, it is worth making the extra effort required to get to **Royal Bardia National Park**, reached by air via the Terai town of **Nepalganj** in the far west. Due to its easy accessibility, Chitwan is in danger of overcrowding, whereas the 968 sq km (374 sq miles) of

Sunset on the Karnali River

Bardia remains virtually untouched. The main attraction here is the variety of bird and animal life, including the wild elephant, swamp deer, blue bull and ghoral that do not occur in Chitwan. Baiting is still permitted in Bardia National Park, making it one of the best places to see the Royal Bengal tiger. Also found at the park are the leopard, rhinoceros, sambar, chital, wild boar, Rhesus and Langur monkeys, Gharial and Marsh Mugger crocodiles and Gangetic dolphins.

This part of the western Terai is the home of the most colourful group of **Tharu**, the collective name given to the original animistic people who farm, hunt and fish in the *dun* (valleys) of Nepal's lowlands. Adorned with magnificent silver jewellery, brilliantly coloured skirts and navy-tattooed ankles, the proud women of the Dangaura Tharu live in unique longhouses. Accommodating as many as 30 families and their livestock, these intriguing mud buildings shelter under huge grass roofs and owe little to the modern world. Divided into rooms by large moulded vats of grain, the inhabitants' belongings hang in baskets from the roof.

Explore the forests and *phantas* (short grasslands) of this beautiful national park by elephant, jeep and on foot, and travel by boat on the massive **Karnali River**, which spills out through its narrow gorge onto the plains of the Terai. One of the great wilderness experiences for the intrepid traveller is the four-day white-water trip down the **Bheri River**. Fishing for **mahseer**, the mighty sport fish of the Himalaya, is at its best in February and March when the snow-fed waters are clear. Photographed and weighed, the catch is then released to fight another day.

It's possible to organise this trip yourself and stay at budget lodges near the park but the most comfortable way to do it is with **Tiger Tops** (tel: 01-411225). They will book the 45-minute flight to Nepalganj where you are met and escorted on the two-hour drive through the villages and jungles to Bardia. **Tiger Tops Karnali Lodge**, with its timber and thatch roofs, terraces and 12 comfortable rooms, is on the edge of the park, adjacent to the Tharu villages. The **Karnali Tented Camp** stretches along the banks of the Karnali River, tucked away within the forest and evoking days of the Raj with its safari tents and attentive service.

Fishing for Mahseer

Sun Koshi gorge, on the road to Tibet

19. A Walk on the Wild Side of Tibet

If regulations permit it may be possible to organise this adventurous trip. Drive to the Tibet border town of Zhangmu (Khasa) and stay overnight in the Zhangmu Hotel. Drive up the gorge to Nyalam, through the Himalayan range and onto the Tibetan plateau. Cross two spectacular passes to Tingri for a wonderful view of the mountains, including the peaks of Everest and Cho Oyu. Return to Khasa for the night. On the following day return to Kathmandu, stopping for lunch at the Dhulikhel Mountain Resort.

It must be stressed that this is a tough trip due to the altitude and can be very difficult to operate owing to a number of circumstances. The Chinese visa regulations for Tibet are subject to change, but at the moment visas are only granted to a tour group of at least five, and require several days' stay in Kathmandu to secure (it is strongly recommended that you book the tour before travelling to Nepal, so that visas can be arranged in advance; some companies insist on it); secondly, the Chinese, who do not permit vehicles to cross the border, may not be able to supply vehicles of their own; and thirdly, the road between Kathmandu and the Tibetan plateau is not infrequently blocked by either landslides (in summer) or snow (in winter). Even if all these conditions are favourable, the cost of the venture may deter some travellers.

You may wonder why I have included it at all. The reason is that, despite these deterents, this trip is so stunning, the variety of scenery so spectacular and the change in cultures and climes so extraordinary that I would urge anyone to move heaven and earth to give it a try.

Start by checking all the various imponderables with your travel agent in Thamel (**Tibet Travels & Tours**, tel: 01-294140, is an experienced operator of tours to Tibet). Make sure you have a re-entry visa to Nepal as well as a Chinese visa for Tibet. Equip yourselves with warm clothes, as the winds on the arid Tibet plateau will be cold throughout the year. Take sunglasses, suncream and scarves to protect yourself from the glare and the dust. Buy extra food and chocolate to sustain you in case you don't like what the hotel offers.

Tibetan family

Although in one day's drive you travel from Zhangmu at 2,112m (6,930ft) to the highest pass over 5,000m (16,000ft), because you return to sleep at Zhangmu at the end of the day there is little danger of full-blown altitude sickness. However, you may find you suffer temporary symptoms such as giddiness, headaches and nausea. To help minimise such ill effects be sure to take with you plenty of liquid to drink (but not alcohol) and move slowly and cautiously in the high, thin air.

The drive on the **Arniko Highway** to the border will take you about four hours. The route is very beautiful, winding through the terraced hills and the great valleys of the **Sunkoshi River** and its tributary, the **Bhote Koshi**. Set off early for this trip, bring along a packed lunch, and be prepared for delays at the border. On the way you will pass through the Nepali towns of **Barabise** and **Tatopani** where you will notice remnants of landslides. Nepal immigration is at **Kodari**, and soon after, the first Chinese soldiers on the **Friendship Bridge** come into view. The no-man's-land between the Nepal checkpost and entry into Tibet on the edge of the sprawling trading depot of **Zhangmu** (also known confusingly as **Khasa**) is a steep hillside above the Bhote Koshi. The **Zhangmu Hotel** is immediately after the checkpost on the left. Also confusing is the fact that Chinese time is two hours and 15 minutes ahead of Nepalese time.

Leave as early as you can the next morning and be prepared for one of the most extraordinary journeys of your life. There is something magical about leaving the lush Nepalese alpine scenery, penetrating the Himalayan range through the spectacular, deep gorge of the Bhote Koshi, and emerging into another world, that of ancient Tibet. You are now in the rain shadow, north of the white peaks of the great mountains that only yesterday you had seen from the south. Guarded by ruined *dzongs* (forts), the arid plateau is tilled by yaks, while nomads tend their herds of sheep and goats and the medieval-looking villages of Tibet huddle against the harsh glare of the elements.

North of the small town of **Nyelam**, perched at the head of the gorge, is the village of **Zhonggang** and the recently rebuilt cave monastery of **Phenkyeling**. This is said to be one of the cave retreats of Milarepa, the 11th-century hermit. The road climbs across two passes, the **Thong La** (5,124m/16,811ft) and the **Lalung La** (5,050m/16,665ft), both crowned with stone *chortens* (cairns) and prayer flags, proffered in thanks for a safe journey.

View from Phenkyeling

The dramatic vista of the many-coloured mountains unfolds in a breathtaking panorama. **Xixabangma** (8,012m/26,286ft), which is also known as **Gosainthan**, is the only 8,000-m (26,000-ft) mountain that is completely within Tibet, and can be seen to the west. After reaching the stone village of **Tingri**, you will be able to see the north faces of **Everest** (8,848m/ 29,029ft) and **Cho Oyu** (8,201m/ 26,906ft) across the plains against a cobalt sky. From here it is another two days' to **Lhasa**.

After spending a second night at the Zhangmu Hotel, return as soon as Chinese and Nepalese border formalities can be completed. Lunch in the comparative sophistication of the **Dhulikhel Mountain Resort**, amidst the green and gold of Nepal's countryside. From here it is barely an hour's journey back to Kathmandu – and the 'real world'.

A pleasant alternative, if logistics and permissions to Tibet are not forthcoming, is to drive from Kathmandu down the Arniko Highway as far as you wish towards the Tibetan border, winding through beautiful terraced hills and great valleys. Return to spend the night in the private chalets of the Dhulikhel Mountain Resort (tel: 01-420774) enjoying the stunning views, peaceful walks and quiet comfort that this penultimate line establishment has to offer.

Right, a Tibetan drukpa, nomad

Eating Out

Unlike other Asian countries, Nepali cuisine is nothing to write home about. Based on similar culinary principles as north Indian cooking, the ordinary people of Nepal live on rice, *dahl* (lentils), curried vegetables and eat meat usually only during festivals. True Nepali specialities are found only in private houses, so be sure to accept an invitation if offered. It is curious that Nepal's isolation did not spawn more regional specialities, especially as the Kathmandu Valley produces such superb vegetables in its fertile fields. However, there are now many restaurants that serve Nepali and Newari food, though their menus are usually combined with Indian or Tibetan dishes.

Other cuisines on offer, including Chinese, Japanese, Thai, Italian and English. Prices in Nepal are generally much lower than elsewhere. Outside Kathmandu and Patan it is difficult to find appealing food, so on a day outing carry something from the bakeries or delicatessens, or a packed lunch from your hotel.

Produced in Nepal are a variety of alcoholic drinks including good beer, rum and vodka and more dubious gin, whisky and brandy. Try the local *raksi* (distilled rice or wheat) or *chhang* (fermented grain, usually barley or millet) if offered in a private house. Imported wines are available only at the hotels and better restaurants, at often prohibitive prices. Bottled soft drinks such as Coke and Pepsi, and mineral water are widely available.

A drink in the bars of Thamel before dinner is always fun if you wish to people-watch – try the **Rum Doodle** or any other bars in this area for trekkers and climbers. Otherwise nightlife is minimal, despite a couple of desultory discotheques in the hotels. Restaurants rarely stay open after 10.30pm – except the casinos at **Annapurna**, **Everest**, **Soalti Crowne Plaza** and **Yak & Yeti** hotels, which never close.

For some of the excursions in this book we've recommended you take a packed lunch. Your hotel should be able to pack one for you but it's easy enough to do it yourself as there are several delis and numerous bakeries in Kathmandu.

Price categories aim to give you a general idea of how restaurants compare to each other, but eating out is very cheap in Nepal and it's difficult to spend over US$20 on even the most sophisticated meal.

Restaurants in Kathmandu

Nepali and Indian

BAITHAK $$$$
Baber Mahal Revisited
Tel: 01-253337
Set in a grand long gallery lined with the portraits of past Ranas this is a very impressive restaurant. The menu features 'delicacies from the Rana court'; the Maharaja's Feast is recommended.

Apples and oranges in Patan

BHOJAN GRIHA $$$$
Dilli Bazaar
Tel: 01-411603
Set in an old building, Nepali cuisine is served accompanied by an entertaining cultural show.

BUKHARA $$$
Hotel Soaltee Crowne Plaza, Tahachal
Tel: 01-272550,
email: crowneplaza@shicp.com.np
Best known for its excellent tandoori cuisine, this is one of the best Indian restaurants in Nepal.

GHAR-E-KABAB $$
Hotel de l'Annapurna, Durbar Marg
Tel: 01-221711
Specialises in the rich cuisine of North India; and there's live sitar music in the evening. You may need to book a table in advanced as the restaurant is justifiably popular.

TANSEN $$
Durbar Marg
Tel: 01-224707
Tasty Indian food served in copper plates and bowls. Optional traditional Nepali seating with tables on pillows on the floor.

KRISHNARPAN $$$$
Hotel Dwarika's, Batisputali
Tel: 01-470770
A wonderful dining experience. Traditional Newari cuisine served in a beautifully decorated restaurant.

NAACHGHAR $$
Hotel Yak & Yeti
Tel: 01-248999
Nepali and Indian dishes served in a beautiful neo-classical ballroom. There's a cultural show most evenings.

TUKCHE THAKALI KITCHEN $
Durbar Marg
Tel: 01-225890
This little restaurant serves authentic Thakali cuisine in an intimate setting. The Thakalis come from the Annapurna region of Nepal and are well known for their hospitality. The set meals here are very good value.

Tibetan

LHASA KITCHEN $$
Hotel Tibet, Lazimpat
Tel: 01-429085
Authentic Tibetan cuisine served in an attractively decorated dining room.

UTSE $
Hotel Utse, Thamel
Tel: 01-228952
Ridiculously cheap Tibetan fare is served in the popular long-running restaurant at this Tibetan-run hotel.

Thai

KRUA THAI $$
Thamel
Tel: 01-414291
Good Thai food served in a restaurant with a pleasant, if loud, ambience. You can dine in the garden or on the roof terrace.

YIN YANG $
Thamel
Tel: 01-425510
A Thai chef prepares the dishes served in this excellent restaurant. Western food, as well as Thai, is available.

Japanese

FUJI $
Kantipath
Tel: 01-225272
Authentic Japanese food in a picturesque Rana cottage complete with stucco columns and a moat. Closed Monday.

KOTO $
Durbar Marg
Tel: 01-226025
Small restaurant serving good-value Japanese cuisine.

Chinese

IMPERIAL PAVILION $$
Hotel Malla, Lekhnath Marg
Tel: 01-410966
Szechwan and Cantonese dishes. The chef is from Szechwan.

Continental

AL FRESCO RESTAURANT $$$
Hotel Soaltee Crowne Plaza, Tahachal
Tel: 01-273999

Italian cuisine in a lively café atmosphere. Pizzas and puddings are especially good.

CHEZ CAROLINE $$
Baber Mahal Revisited
Tel: 01-263070
Located amongst the stylish boutiques of Baber Mahal Revisited, this authentic French salon de thé and patisserie is perfect for a light lunch or tea. Their crème caramel and mousse au chocolat are irresistably superb.

FIRE & ICE PIZZERIA $
Tridevi Marg, Thamel
Tel: 01-250210
This Italian-run café serves superb pizza, home-made ice cream, and wine by the glass. Good value for money and justifiably popular.

HOTEL VAJRA $$
Bijeswori, Swayambhu
Tel: 01-271545
Recommended for the views over Kathmandu, *à la carte* lunches and dinners are served at the two roof-top bars here.

KC'S RESTAURANT AND BAMBOOZE BAR $
Thamel
Tel: 01-414387
An old favourite Thamel hangout which retains its atmosphere and value. The 'sizzler' was invented here 25 years ago.

KILROY'S OF KATHMANDU $$$
Thamel

Brass pots sell by the weight

Tel: 01-250440
Run by an Irish chef, this restaurant is one of the best in Thamel. You can dine in the garden or in the comfortable dining room; there's also a café. There's an imaginative menu, and Irish stew and Guinness are both available.

K@MANDU CYBERMATHA TEA HOUSE
Kantipath
Tel: 01-256079
The city's best cybercafé, with networked terminals connected to the Internet via a high speed digital link. Drinks and snacks are served.

MIKE'S BREAKFAST $
Naxal
Tel: 01-424303
Started by an ex-Peace Corps volunteer, Mike's Breakfast is a long-running restaurant that now also serves lunch and dinner (in season) as well as their excellent American breakfasts. The food is Western or Mexican and you can sit indoors or out.

RUM DOODLE $
Thamel
Tel: 01-414336
Good-value food is served in this classic mountaineers' pub.

SIMPLY SHUTTERS BISTRO $$$
Baber Mahal Revisited
Tel: 01-259015
Well-presented French bistro cuisine. Open daily for lunch and dinner.

GURKHA GRILL $$$
Soaltee Crowne Plaza Kathmandu
Tel: 01-272550
Kathmandu's finest French restaurant, with both classic and nouvelle cuisine.

CHIMNEY ROOM $$$$
Hotel Yak & Yeti
Tel: 01-248999
The restaurant on which The Chimney was based was started by the legendary Boris Lissanevitch, the White Russian emigré who pioneered tourism in Nepal. As you might expect, borscht and chicken Kiev are both on the menu.

Kathmandu is a treasure trove of opportunities for shoppers, but beware of the cheap trinkets that tend to look like the junk they are when you return home. It is expected that you will bargain, except in the smart shops, and even then it is worth a try. As a general rule, if you like it and can afford it, buy it – you may never find the same thing again. The main shops are in **Thamel**, **Durbar Marg** and **Jawalikhel** but you will find temptations wherever you go.

The chic boutiques of **Baber Mahal Revisited** are a recent addition to the shopping scene in Kathmandu. Part of this grand Rana palace has been restored to a very high standard and the seven courtyards now house 40 upmarket shops and restaurants. Even if you're just window shopping, Baber Mahal Revisited is well worth seeing for the setting alone.

Look out for shops which benefit the craftspeople more directly: the **Mahaguthi** shops, one in Patan and one in Durbar Marg, for example. **Dhukuti** and **Hastakala** (handicrafts) specialise in crafts made by disadvantaged groups; proceeds go to charity. In Patan, near the Kumbeshwar Temple, the **Kumbeshwar Technical School** provides training and employment for low caste and untouchable Nepalis. The carpets, sweaters and woodwork sold here are of a very high quality.

Metalwork

Patan craftsmen are famous for their metalwork, and silver and goldsmiths ply their trade using tools and methods that have hardly changed in centuries. Brass candlesticks are also a good buy. Especially interesting is the 'lost wax' method of casting bronze which can be seen in Patan at **Nepalese Crafts** and **Mahabaudha Bidyadhari Silpa Bhandar** on the Patan Industrial Estate.

Woodcarving

The Newars are famous for their skills in woodcarving. There are beautifully-ornate lattice panels and carvings in the form of traditional window photo frames. The **Woodcarving Studio** in Jawalakhel, Patan is interesting to visit.

Carpets

Now the basis of a major industry, these beautiful handmade wool carpets are world famous and good value in Nepal, as you might expect. Most measure 1 by 2 metres (3ft by 6ft) and reflect traditional Tibetan designs. The best are made from 100 percent Tibetan wool but most are blended with wool from New Zealand. The

Wooden masks and household implements

soft pastel colours are very popular, though not 'naturally dyed' as the shop-keepers would have you believe.

Choose from a dazzling selection from the shops in **Jawalakhel**, or **Thamel**. There are some superb examples at **Red Thread** and **Tharu Tiger Carpets** in Baber Mahal.

You can also buy rugs from Kashmir from the Indian carpet sellers in **Thamel**.

Pashmina Shawls

Wool and mixed wool shawls make excellent gifts. They are available from shops in Thamel and on Durbar Marg. Made from the finest goat wool, the pure white ones are the most expensive. **Wheels Boutique** in Durbar Marg has a good selection.

Avoid any articles made from shahtoosh. This very fine wool comes from the chiru, an endangered Tibetan antelope that is killed for its fleece.

Jackets and Sweaters

Less fine but quite fun and again good for gifts are the multicoloured sweaters available in Thamel. They need careful handwashing if you want them to last.

You can also buy jackets and waist-coats in a wide range of fabrics and designs. Embroidery is big business and any design you fancy can be embroidered onto a jacket or T-shirt.

Silk

Nepal silk is not yet up to international standards but you will be tempted by the delightful hand-painted Chinese silk outfits, brocades, fabrics and scarfs in the elegant boutiques in **Durbar Marg** and **Keshar Mahal**. Most silk tends to be blended with pashmina.

Gurkha Khukris

Genuine *khukris*, traditional curved knives of Nepal, are hand made by Gurkha soldiers in their army workshops. There's an excellent selection at **Khukuri House**, Sat Ghumti, Thamel. Beware of poor quality imitations being sold on the streets.

Jewellery

No major precious stones are found in Nepal but you will find good silver-work bracelets and tiny animals in traditional Nepali filigree designs, sometimes inlaid with small pieces of coral or turquoise.

The Sherpas and Tibetans value the dark red coral highly. Turquoise should be bright blue-green. Both are traded from Tibet and are not cheap. Look for pretty silver bangles and earrings; unique to Nepal are the plaited bangles of three metals — copper, brass and silver (or iron) — popular with those who suffer from arthritis. Most convenient are the **Durbar Marg** or **New Road** jewellers. In Barber Mahal Revisited there are several exclusive jewellery shops, including the upmarket **Marzan Jewellery**.

Kathmandu's jewellery craftsmen are very skilled. If you've lost a treasured piece of earring, give the remaining one to a jeweller and he'll make you an almost identical copy.

Enjoy making your own combinations of multicoloured glass beads in the **Bead Market**, in Indrachowk.

Paintings

Thangkas are traditional religious scroll paintings that depict Buddhist deities and complex designs. They can take many hours to paint and the price often reflects the amount of work involved in completing them. They are available in many shops but Bhaktapur is one good place to buy them. Look in the shops in **Tamaudi Tole** leading down from the Durbar Square, check for fine detailed work and gold leaf. Also look in the Tibetan shops around **Bodhnath** and in the **Indigo Gallery** above Mike's Restaurant in Naxaul. A traditional Nepali-style *thangka* is known as a *paubha*.

Mithila paintings, from Janakpur in south Nepal, can now be purchased in some shops in Kathmandu. These distinctive paintings often featuring naive or abstract figures and geometric designs are traditionally done by women. The Janakpur Women's Development Centre is encouraging local women to produce Mithila paintings to earn money. In Kathmandu these striking paintings can be bought at the **Mahaguthi** shops in Durbar Marg and Patan.

B B Thapa, in his shop to the right beside the big tree opposite SATA in Jawalakhel, offers an enchanting range of

Puppets and masks in Bhaktapur

Kathmandu Valley and Nepal view paintings in the primitive style that is normally associated with Sherpan or Tibetan fresco painters.

You should also look out for the attractive watercolours now being sold in shops in **Patan**.

Antiques and Art Objects

Kathmandu is a mecca for collectors. Glory in a galaxy of superb old Tibetan carpets, precious *thangkas*, Chinese embroideries, porcelain and jade, Bhutanese dress pieces, coral and turquoise jewellery, gold and silver ritual art objects and fine Nepali bronzes.

It is no longer easy to find bargains and prices tend to be index-linked. Be aware of the local restrictions for exporting, which require certificates for some antiques; get the shopkeeper to help you. It is illegal to export objects over 100 years old.

Recommended are the **Tibet Ritual Art Gallery** and the **Potala Gallery** on the first floors in Durbar Marg, **Curio Arts** also in Durbar Marg, and **Tamrakar Antiques** in Baber Mahal Revisited; but keep your eyes open in Bodhnath.

Books

Kathmandu is, perhaps surprisingly, a very good place to buy English-language books. You'll find all the current bestsellers available for less than half what they sell for in the West. This is also probably the best place to buy books on Tibet and Tibetan Buddhism.

Mandala Book Point, Kantipath, has a wide range as does **Pilgrims**, near the Kathmandu Guest House in Thamel.

Handmade Paper

Traditional handmade paper goods make excellent souvenirs since they are very light. The paper is made from the *lokta* bark. When it was first marketed to tourists all you could buy were writing pads and cards made from this rough paper. Now there's a wonderful range of goods, from photograph albums with bright bindings to colourful stationery, beautiful lampshades and decorative boxes.

Several shops in Thamel sell nothing but paper. For the highest quality handmade paper goods, however, visit **Paper Moon** in Baber Mahal Revisited.

Tea

The main tea growing district in Nepal is in the east, around Ilam. Many shops in Kathmandu sell Ilam tea and it can make an excellent present to take home, often sold in attractive silk pouches.

Topis

The *topis* (caps) that many Nepalis wear come in two varieties; plain black and multicoloured. Their asymmetric shape is said to be reminiscent of Mount Kailash, the peak in western Tibet that is holy for both Buddhists and Hindus.

Topis make good souvenirs and are widely available in Kathmandu Valley. Near the Thamel restaurant, Fire & Ice Pizzeria, there's a shop that specialises in nothing else.

Other Handicrafts

One positive aspect of the tourist boom in Nepal is the improvement in the quality of locally-made handicrafts. There are colourful handspun fabrics on sale everywhere; and multicoloured masks and dancing puppets can be found in Bhaktapur.

You might also want to take a look at some of the terracotta animals in the pottery village of Thimi, although you would need to be very taken by them to carry them home.

Calendar of Special Events

Nepal is known as the land of festivals. Here, in the shadow of the mountain gods, celebrations are so frequent that the festivals often overlap each other. There are more than 50 such occasions a year, with as many as 120 days set aside to be observed. Most are linked to one or both of the country's great religions, Hinduism and Buddhism. Nepali's celebrate enthusiastically, and you are welcome to take part.

Festival dates vary from year to year because of the lunar calendar. Many are determined only after complex astrological calculations and as some festivals take place over a period of several days, it is usually difficult to know in advance which day festivities will take place, or where. The uncertainty is even considered part of the mystery.

This list will give you a guideline, but you should check dates with your hotel or travel agent when you arrive in Kathmandu.

Royal escort accompanies the king

MAGH (JANUARY/FEBRUARY)

Magh Sankranti. Marked with ritual bathing, even though it often falls on the coldest day of the year, this festival marks the passing of the inauspicious winter month of Pousch and rejoices that spring is at hand.

Maha Snan. Celebrates the holy bath given to Shiva, when he is bathed in yoghurt and honey and dressed anew.

Basant Panchami. The Festival of Spring is also the festival of Saraswati, goddess of learning. Students about to take exams and hundreds of devotees flock to the Saraswati shrine at Swayambhunath. The king attends ceremonies at Hanuman Dhoka to pray for a good harvest. The most auspicious day to get married or to introduce children to the alphabet.

Magh Purnima. The full moon (*purnima*) marks the beginning of the month in which Parvati is worshipped at her shrines.

PHALGUN (FEBRUARY/MARCH)

Shivaratri. This great festival celebrating the birthday of Shiva is the time to be at Pashupatinath. A colourful crowd of literally thousands of devotees, *yogis* and *sadhus*, or holy ascetics, from all over the Indian subcontinent gather to line up to make offerings to Lord Pashupati, keep a night time vigil with bonfires and bathe at dawn in the Bagmati River.

Democracy Day or **King Tribhuvan Jayanti**. The statue of King Tribhuvan is garlanded in a procession to Tripureshwar.

Losar or **Tibetan New Year**. One of the most beautiful festivals, usually coincides within a few days of Chinese New Year. The third day of the otherwise family and house-oriented holiday is the time for celebrating at Bodhnath. Everyone dresses in their best clothes and jewellery and joins in the celebrations where new prayer flags are hung, the Dalai Lama's portrait paraded and one of the great moments of the year takes place as hundreds of Tibetans throw *tsampa* or barley flour into the air accompanied by a great roar of welcome to

Losar at Bodhnath

the New Year. Dancing takes place in the evening at monasteries around the stupa at Bodhnath.

Holi or **Phagu**. Kathmandu Durbar Square is where this rowdy festival of colour and fertility is celebrated with the raising of a 7.5m (25ft) *chir* or bamboo pole, decked with streamers, burned at the end of the week. Wear old clothes as you are most likely to be sprayed with coloured water by over enthusiastic kids.

CHAITRA MARCH/APRIL

Seto or Rath. For four days during early evening, the guardian deity of the Seto (White) Machhendra is pulled in a towering chariot through the streets of Kathmandu. The vehicle which stands on wheels 1.8m (6ft) in diameter is finally transported back to the shrine at Asan Tole on a small palanquin. Before this, on each night, the chariot stops at specific places where residents tend to the image.

Ghorajatra. Celebrated by horse races and gymnastics attended by the king, this horse festival has become a military pageant and draws crowds to the Tundhikhel.

Pase Chare. Coincides with Ghorajatra. After the horsemanship displays, the demon Gurumpa is carried to the Tundhikhel in a midnight procession.

Chaitra Dasain. Ritual offerings and sacrifices are made to Durga, exactly six months away from her great festival of Desain.

BAISAKH
APRIL/MAY

Bisket. Bhaktapur is the place to be for this exciting and rousing festival which lasts for a week and celebrates the slaying of two demon serpents. A frenetic tug of war at dusk determines who shall have the honour of dragging a huge chariot conveying Bhadrakali and Bhairav through the streets of the city. Spectacular masked dancing and the felling of a long pole, commemorating victory during the great battle of Mahabharata mark the beginning of the Nepalese New Year.

Bal Kumari Jatra. The New Year is marked at Thimi with torch-lit processions honouring the Bal Kumari, a consort of Bhairav.

New Year prayer flags, Bodhnath

Mata Tirtha Shan or **Mothers' Day**. Persons whose mothers have died during the year must ritually bathe at this temple near Thankot. Living mothers are offered gifts.

Buddha Jayanti. Lord Buddha's birthday is celebrated at all Buddhist shrines, particularly Bodhnath and Swayambhunath.

JESHTHA
MAY/JUNE

Sithinakha or **Kumar Shasthi**. Jaisedewal, south of Kathmandu Durbar Square, will be thronged with people celebrating the birthday of Kumar, son of Shiva.

Seto Machhendranath Festival

ASHADH
JUNE/JULY

Tulsi Bijropan. This women's festival of fasting and purification involves planting the sacred *tulsi* plant, a close relative of common basil.

Gokarana Aunshi or **Fathers' Day**. Celebrated by ritual bathing at the Gokarna Mahadev for those whose fathers have died in the past year. Living fathers are honoured with gifts.

SHRAWAN
JULY/AUGUST

Bhoto Jatra. Astrologers fix the exact time. The culmination of the several-month long procession of the Rato (Red) Machhendranath chariot since it set off from Pulchowk in April, this important Patan festival is designed to ensure a good monsoon for crops.

The bejewelled waistcoat or *bhoto*, supposedly belonging to the serpent king, is displayed at Jawalakhel in the presence of the royal family. Once every 12 years (the next time is 2003) the chariot is dragged painstakingly all the way to Bungamati.

Ghanta Karna. The Night of the Devil is traditionally the last day for rice planting. The evil demon was outwitted by a frog and children collect coins to pay for his funeral.

Nag Panchami. *Nagas*, or the sacred serpents, are worshipped and pictures can be seen displayed above many doorways.

Raksha Bandhan or **Janai Purnima**. Every Brahman and Chhetri must renew their *munja*, or sacred thread on this day after first taking a ritual bath in holy water.

The Kumbeshwar Temple in Patan is the place to be, as the water in the tanks there supposedly come from the sacred Gosainkund Lake, high in Helambu. The beautiful gold and silver *linga*, usually kept in the temple, are displayed on this day on a platform in the middle of the tank, reached only along a narrow plank.

Gai Jatra. An epic love of a king and queen is celebrated in this festival, which is more like a carnival. Families in which deaths have occurred in the previous year will send cows or children dressed as cows to frolic and sing in the Durbar Squares of Kathmandu, Patan and Bhaktapur to assist their deceased's entry into heaven.

Newari New Year

Krishna Jayanti. Birthday of the beloved god Krishna is celebrated in Patan Durbar Square.

BHADRA
AUGUST/SEPTEMBER

Tij. This colourful women's festival has groups of red sari-clad ladies singing in high spirits in the streets on their way to ritually bathe in the Bagmati River at Pashupatinath.

Indrajatra. Probably the most spectacular of all Valley festivals. Torch-lit processions and dancing to honour Indra, the god of rain, are held in this eight-day celebration which centres on the Kathmandu Durbar Square.

On the third day the *Kumari*, or Living Goddess, is paraded in a special chariot and worshipped by the king himself. Masks of Bhairav decorate the city and local beer pours forth from the mouths of these masks to refresh the local revellers.

ASHWIN
SEPTEMBER/OCTOBER

Dasain or **Durga Puja**. This 10-day festival is celebrated all over Nepal, honouring bountiful fertility and the conquest of evil. Normal life comes to a standstill as everyone attends to his religious and family duties.

On *Phulpati*, the day of flowers, there is a procession to Hanuman Dhoka attended by the king. On the eighth and ninth days there are massive numbers of ritual animal sacrifices, for every tool that is used during the year must be blessed. Shrines all over the country literally run with blood. On the final day the palace is opened for all who wish to line up to receive a *tika* from the hands of the king or queen.

Gai Jatra

Tihar, or **Diwali**, and **Lakshmi Puja**. The Festival of Lights starts with honouring the crow, the dog and the cow. The fourth day coincides with Newari New Year. On the fourth and fifth evenings Laksmi, the goddess of wealth and prosperity, is enticed into the home by lights. Thousands of oil lamps and candles adorn doors, windows and balconies. Brothers are feted by their sisters on the last day and honoured with elaborate *tikas* and garlands.

Haribodhini Ekadasi. This most auspicious *Ekadasi* (the 11th day of each lunar fortnight, there are 24 in a year) welcomes Vishnu back from his long summer sleep. Join worshippers at Budhanilkanth where festivities cul-

minate as fasting devotees conclude the pilgrimage to his temples of Changu Narayan, Bisankhu Narayan, Sekh Narayan and Ichangu Narayan.
HM The Queen's Birthday. The queen receives a procession of well-wishers who visit the palace at Durbar Marg.

MARGA/MANGSIR
NOVEMBER/DECEMBER

Yomarhi Punhi. The Newari rice festival is celebrated at Panauti, where the family paddy store is blessed and rice cakes called *yomarhi* are prepared.

PAUSH
DECEMBER/JANUARY

Mahendra Jayanti or **Constitution Day**. Garlands are laid on the statue of King Mahendra in Durbar Marg.
Birendra Jayanti (The King's Birthday). Well-wishers at Durbar Marg bring birthday offerings to the king on this national holiday.
Prithvi Jayanti. The statue of King Prithvi Narayan Shah opposite Singha Durbar is garlanded and his photograph paraded through the city.

Festival dancing

Practical Information

When to Visit

October to April is the best time to visit Nepal. However, being the most popular, this is also the most crowded time. The cold clear winter months of December and January are good for mountain views, despite misty mornings and an invigorating evening chill. However, trekking at higher altitudes can be impossible from January through February, as passes may be blocked by snow and there is a danger of avalanches.

The next busiest, and in many ways the best months to visit, are February and March with spring flowers and gentle temperatures. Late April and May can be hot and hazy and it is best to avoid the monsoon rains from June to September if you are planning to trek or visit the lowland national parks.

In the Valley, however, this can be one of the prettiest times with only intermittent rain, lush green rice fields, wonderful light effects and very few other visitors.

Visas and Permits

Visas valid for 60 days can be bought from any Nepalese embassy or consulate or upon arrival at Kathmandu's Tribhuvan airport, the Kodari border with China or Indian border entry points for US$30 (or local currency equivalent). To avoid unnecessary delay, be sure you have passport-sized photographs and the right change.

All tourist visas can be extended at the Department of Immigration in New Baneswar, Kathmandu tel: 01-494273 (open 9am–5pm Monday to Friday, but applications must be submitted before midday). Visas may be extended for up to four months, and each extra month will cost you US$50.

If you are planning to leave and return, be sure to ask for a multi-entry visa, which will cost you an additional US$25–60. Trek permits are no longer necessary for most trekking areas in Nepal. To travel to a remote or restricted area, you must use a registered trekking agent to make arrangements – they will process the permits as part of the service.

Vaccinations

Typhoid, hepatitis, rabies and meningitis are among the vaccinations recommended. Make sure your routine tetanus, diphtheria and polio inoculations are up to date. Yellow fever vaccinations are essential if arriving from an infected area. Cholera shots are not required. Others are only

Downtown Kathmandu

A departure tax of Rs 1,000 is charged per person on all international flights except flights to SAARC countries, where a tax of Rs 900 is payable. A tax of Rs 100 is levied on domestic flights.

GETTING ACQUAINTED

Government and Geography

Nepal is a constitutional monarchy headed by His Majesty King Birendra Bir Bikram Shah Dev. Following demonstrations and riots, the palace announced on 8 April 1990 the lifting of the legal ban on political parties and on 9 November 1990 a new constitution was proclaimed.

In Nepal's first decade of democracy the country has been ruled by several short-lived coalitions and continuously changing prime ministers. Political infighting often leads to upheavals and demonstrations in the capital. Another problem involves the gradual spread to the centre of a terrorist campaign led by a Maoist rebel faction based in impoverished western Nepal.

The King (born 28 December 1945) and Queen Aishwarya Rajya Lakshmi Devi Shah (born 7 November 1949) have three children; the older, His Royal Highness Crown Prince Dipendra (born 27 June 1971) is heir to the throne. Nepal is the only Hindu monarchy in the world.

Nepal's population is extremely young: fifty percent of the 23 million population of Nepal are under the age of 21. The population is growing at an annual rate of 2.5 percent. Around 80 percent are dependent on agriculture. For subsistence farmers, industriously carving out a living from small plots on terraced hillsides, the annual per capita income of US$222 is a largely irrelevant figure.

Development is hampered by lack of roads and infrastructure in this largely mountainous land which, in only 160km (100 miles) goes from the highest point on earth, Mount Everest, known in Nepal as Sagarmatha, 8,848m/29,028ft to the lowland Terai less than 100m (350ft) above sea level.

About the same size as England or New Zealand, Nepal stretches 885km (553

necessary in certain areas and at particular times of year. Consult with your GP three months before travelling.

Money Matters

Nepalese rupees (Rs) are the monetary unit and the official rate of exchange fluctuates against other currencies. Check the *Rising Nepal* newspaper, where rates are published daily on the back page.

Money can be changed in the banks and hotels and the exchange counter at the airport. Make sure you keep all Foreign Exchange Encashment Receipts as these are necessary to show proof of currency exchange when changing back excess rupees on departure.

It is illegal to export or import Nepalese currency. All airline, hotel and travel agency payments must be made in foreign exchange by foreigners. American Express, MasterCard and Visa are widely accepted in the Kathmandu Valley.

Clothing

Your wardrobe will depend on what you are planning to do in Nepal, but generally only the most casual clothes are required. Safari-style cottons, modest skirts, jeans and comfortable track shoes are ideal with a warm sweater and jacket for cold winter evenings.

Bring sunglasses for daytime and rely on a local umbrella if it rains, which is seldom except during the monsoon season. If you are trekking or river running, consult an equipment list from your trekking agency for specialist gear.

Electricity

Electrical outlets are rated at 220 volts/50 cycles though some fluctuation is not unusual. Power cuts are common. Big hotels have their own generators. Bring a small flashlight.

miles) from east to west and has a total land area of 145,391 sq km (56,139 sq miles).

Health care and literacy figures are amongst the world's worst and Nepal is largely dependent on foreign aid for its economic development. Tourism and hand-made wool carpet exports are the largest foreign exchange earners.

Kathmandu, the capital, is at an altitude of 1,350m (4,400ft) and has a population of about 600,000, with almost one million people making the Kathmandu Valley their home.

Climate

Nepal has an extreme variety of climates, from the eternal snows of the Himalaya to the tropical lowlands.

Few capitals enjoy as many hours of sunshine as the Kathmandu Valley, which has three seasons:

Winter: October to March, 10°–25°C (50°–77°F), with cold nights dropping to almost freezing and a morning mist due to the rapidly rising daytime temperatures. Clear sparkling sunny days.
Spring: April to mid-June, 11°–30°C (52°–86°F), with warm, sometimes hazy days and occasional evening thunder storms, the nights are pleasantly cool.
Monsoon: June to September, 19°–36°C (66°–97°F), intermittent violent downpours (often only at night) create some flooding and landslides, and keep the temperature down and the humidity high.

Time

Nepal is five hours 45 minutes ahead of GMT and 15 minutes ahead of Indian Standard Time.

Calendars

Five different calendars are used simultaneously in Nepal. The official one used by the government is the lunar Bikram Samat calendar which started counting the days on 23 Feb 57 BC. Hence 1999 is 2056 of the Bikram era. However, the familiar Gregorian calendar is widely used. Traditional calendars include the Nepal Samat, established in AD879–880, the Shaka Samat, established AD77, and the

Tibetan calendar, Bhot Byalo, established in 127BC.

The Nepalese fiscal year which begins in mid-July, is 365 days long with 12 months ranging in length from 29 to 32 days, depending on solar movement. These months are: Baisakh (31 days), Jestha (31 days), Asadh (32 days), Shrawan (32 days), Bhadra (31 days), Ashwin (30 days), Kartik (30 days), Marga (29 days), Paush (30 days), Magh (29 days), Phalgun (30 days), Chaitra (30 days).

Hours of Business

Government offices are open from 9am to 5pm, Monday to Friday for most of the year. They close at 4pm during the three winter months and 3pm on Fridays.

Banks open at 10am and close at 3pm Monday to Friday. Many private businesses and shops operate on a six day week. Shops seldom open before 10am but don't normally close until 8 or 9pm.

Culture and Customs

Although every visitor is immediately struck by the charm and smiling friendliness of the Nepali people, avoid inadvertently offending your hosts and keep the following in mind. Both men and women can go about almost everywhere with confidence but keep your wallet out of sight and your bag zipped up.

If you are approached or hassled by the curious, smiling patiently usually gets better results from these proud people than losing your cool. Rarely do people mind being photographed, but it is polite to stop if they do.

Nepalis are on the whole very tolerant

Book a tour

of tourist behaviour, but respect in temples and shrines is expected – be ready to remove your shoes. The traditional greeting, *Namaste*, literally translated as 'I salute all divine qualities in you', should be spoken while folding the hand in front of the chest. The king, once regarded as an incarnation of the Hindu god, Vishnu, is still treated with genuine reverence so all references to the royal family must be suitably respectful.

Never point with a finger and especially not with your feet, never touch the top of anyone's head and never give or receive anything in your left 'polluted' hand – best is to offer and receive with both hands.

Tipping

It is customary to tip about 10 percent in restaurants, hotels and taxis (who have been particularly helpful). Small favours should be tipped with 20 rupees. Travel and trekking guides are usually tipped much more. Refrain from giving sweets and money to every child who asks.

Tourist Information and Maps

The detailed *Insight Guide: Nepal* is widely available in the many bookshops in Kathmandu town. The informative up-to-date *Nepal Traveller* magazine may be handed to you free at the airport upon arrival.

GETTING AROUND

Private Cars

The most convenient, reliable and time-effective way to get around is with a private car and an experienced guide (you are not allowed to drive yourself), which can be booked through a travel agent or arranged through your hotel. If you stay within the rim of the Valley, it will cost you about US$70 for the whole day. If you are satisfied with the service, a Rs 150 tip is customary.

Taxis

Taxis are widely available and much cheaper than private cars. They have black registration plates with white numbers, (private cars have white numbers on red plates). Make sure their meters are working.

Bicycles

A great way to see the Valley is by bicycle, especially on mountain bikes, which are ideal for exploring the dirt roads of the Valley. Steer clear of the busy main roads, however, as pollution is becoming an increasing problem. Mountain bikes (now widely available in Thamel) are worth paying more for. Check that the brakes and bell work.

Walking

You should be prepared to do a lot of walking if you want to taste the real flavour of the Valley, absorb its people, their culture and way of life. Most of the interesting sights have to be reached and explored on foot. Leave the busy main roads and stroll at a leisurely pace through the rice and mustard fields. You can expect to be safe everywhere you go and will find the Nepalese people even more friendly off the beaten track.

Public Transport

Buses, trams, three-wheeled scooters (*tempos*) and bicycle-rickshaws all ply the streets of Kathmandu. They are all slow, noisy and fairly uncomfortable but they are a cheap way of getting around.

WHERE TO STAY

The prices below do not include the 10 percent service charge, 10 percent tourist tax, or 2 percent VAT. The star ratings awarded by the Department of Tourism are quantitative rather than qualitative, and this list is by no means exhaustive. There

Decked out in wedding finery

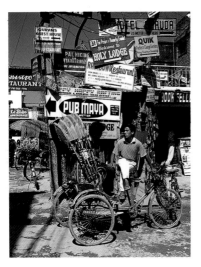

are plenty of lodges and guesthouses for less than US$10 to choose from in Thamel. See also hotels, resorts and guesthouses recommended in the itineraries.

The following symbols indicate price ranges for a double room. $=under US$50; $$=US$50–100; $$$=US$100–150.

Kathmandu

Five-star

HOTEL DE L'ANNAPURNA
Durbar Marg, Kathmandu
Tel: 01-221711 Fax: 01-225236;
Email: apurna@taj.mos.com.np
Run by the Taj Group from India, this central hotel was the first five-star in town. 160 rooms, pool, tennis, several restaurants. *$$$*

RADISSON
Lazimpat, Kathmandu
Tel: 01-419358 Fax: 01-411720;
Email: radkat@mos.com.np
Upmarket hotel situated near the Royal Palace. Swimming pool, health centre. *$$$*

SOALTEE HOLIDAY INN CROWNE PLAZA
Tahachal, Kathmandu
Tel: 01-272550 Fax: 01-272205
Email: crowneplaza@shicp.com.np
The best hotel in town, with extensive facilities, good restaurants and spectacular 'regal' suites built for the South Asian (SAARC) Heads of State. *$$$*

Every which way

YAK AND YETI
Durbar Marg, Kathmandu
Tel: 01-248999 Fax: 01-227782
Email: reservation@yakandyeti.com
Excellently located, this historic home of the great Boris Lissanevitch, founder of Nepal's tourism industry, is part Rana palace. Pool, tennis, sauna. *$$$*

DWARIKA'S KATHMANDU VILLAGE
Battisputali, Kathmandu
Tel: 01-470770 Fax: 01-471379
Email: dwarika@mos.com.np
A wonderful Nepali antique woodcarving collection is incorporated into the design of this imaginative family-run hotel. *$$$*

Four-star

HOTEL HIMALAYA
Kupondole, Patan, Kathmandu
Tel: 01-523900 Fax: 01-523909
Email: Himalaya@lalitpur.mos.com.np
Cool white marble, spacious rooms and a swimming pool with a view in this Japanese-owned property. *$$*

MALLA HOTEL
Lekhnath Marg, Kathmandu
Tel: 01-410620, 410968 Fax: 01-418382
Email: malla@htlgrp.mos.com.np
Well placed near the Royal Palace and other sights and well run. Has a charming garden and a restaurant serving the best Chinese food in town. *$$*

HOTEL SHANGRI-LA
Lazimpat
Tel: 01-412999 Fax: 01-414184
Email: hosang@mos.com.np
Lovely brick-built favourite with good food, great service and a glorious garden to ramble around in. *$$*

Three-star

HOTEL MARSHYANGDI
Thamel
Tel: 01-414105 Fax: 01-410008
Email: htlgold@mos.com.np
Conveniently located on the edge of Thamel. Centrally air-conditioned rooms, video and reading room, café, bar and restaurants. *$$*

HOTEL TIBET
Lazimpat
Tel: 01-429085 Fax: 01-410957
Email: hotel@tibet.mos.com.np
A well-managed, hotel with excellent ser-
vice. There's a good Tibetan restaurant. *$$*

SUMMIT HOTEL
Kupondole Heights
Tel: 01-524694 Fax: 01-523737
Email: summit@wlink.com.np
Lovely rooms, view and swimming pool in
this pleasant hotel. Quiet, though not very
conveniently situated. *$$*

Two-star

KATHMANDU GUEST HOUSE
Thamel
Tel: 01-413632 Fax: 01-417133
Email: ktmguest@ecomail.com.np
This is one of the best and certainly the
most famous of the Thamel lodges, and a
favourite with world travellers. Situated
in the heart of the action, it is frequently
fully booked. *$*

MANASLU
Lazimpat
Tel: 01-410071, 413470 Fax: 01-416516
Friendly, quiet and central: a real 'find'. *$*

MUSTANG HOLIDAY INN
Jyatha
Tel: 01-249041 Fax: 01-249016
Email: ntv@mhiwlink.com.np
This is an old favourite: central yet quiet.
Rooftop terrace and garden. *$*

TIBET GUEST HOUSE
Chetrapati
Tel: 01-251763 Fax: 01-260518
Email: tibet@guesths.mos.com.np
Near Thamel. Friendly, helpful and really
excellent value. *$*

HOTEL VAJRA
Bijeswari
Tel: 01-271545 Fax: 01-271695
Email: varja@mos.com.np
More a cultural experience than a hotel.
Attractively designed and with good views
from the rooftop bar. Sauna, library, live
entertainment. *$*

Pokhara Valley

TREK LODGE KER & DOWNEY
Maharajganj
Tel: 061-416751 Fax: 061-410407
Email: nepadv@asia.mos.com.np
Three purpose-built lodges with guided
walks between them. *$$$*

BEGNAS LAKE RESORT & VILLAS
Sundari Danda, Begnas Lake
Tel: 061-29330 Fax: 061-249324
Email: villas@begnas.mos.com.np
Peaceful location 12km (8 miles) from
Pokhara on the lake shore. Rustic rooms,
restaurant, bar. *$$*

FEWA
Lakeside
Tel: 061-20151
Email: mike@fewa.mos.com.np
Basic rooms but an excellent attached
restaurant. Right on the waterfront. *$$$*

Royal Chitwan National Park

MACHAN WILDLIFE RESORT
Reservations: PO Box 3140, Durbar Marg,
Kathmandu.
Tel: 01-225001 Fax: 01-240681
Email: wildlife@machan.mos.com.np
Peaceful location 12km (8 miles) from
Pokhara on the lake shore. Rustic rooms,
restaurant, bar. *$$$*

GREEN MANSIONS
Reservations: Jamal, Kathmandu
Tel: 01-231271 Fax: 01-521057
One of a plethora of small lodges that
have mushroomed on the edge of Chitwan at Sauraha. Peaceful atmosphere and
fishpond. *$$*

Royal Bardia National Park

DOLPHIN MANOR
Reservations: Lazimpat, Kathmandu
Tel: 01-420308 Fax: 01-415401
One of the dozen or so simple lodges scat-
tered around park headquarters at Thakur-
dwara. *$$*

RHINO LODGE
Reservations: Thamel, Kathmandu
Tel: 01-416918 Fax: 01-417146,
Email; rhinotvl@wlink.com.np
Basic but fun. *$$*

HEALTH AND EMERGENCIES

Hygiene

It is not uncommon for minor problems to occur and elementary hygiene precautions are in order. Never drink unboiled and untreated water and do not trust ice cubes anywhere except in the very best hotels. Avoid eating raw vegetables, peel all fruit and do not be tempted to eat anywhere except proper restaurants. Never walk barefoot and wash your hands frequently. 'Traveller's tummy' should clear up after a few days but if it is severe and persistent, or interferes with your travel plans, get a stool test and medical assistance.

Medicine

Most medicines that you are likely to require are readily and cheaply available without a prescription. Look out for the well-known brand names manufactured under licence in India but check the labels carefully as the contents may be different from those you are familiar with at home.

If you fall ill while in Nepal, do not rely on pharmacists when making a diagnosis but get proper medical assistance.

Clinics

There are Nepali doctors attached to all the big hotels. The **Nepal International Clinic** is in Hiti Durbar across from the Royal Palace (tel: 01-435357). Best of all – but more expensive than others – is the American-staffed **CIWEC Clinic** off Durbar Marg, near Hotel Yak and Yeti (tel: 01-228531).

Hospitals

Some Kathmandu hospitals do have English-speaking staff but are not up to international standards. Where feasible, foreign visitors should try to reach the excellent hospital facilities in Bangkok, Thailand.

For accidents and emergencies contact the **CIWEC Clinic** (tel: 01-228531) for advice (they do not have an emergency department but are open 24 hours and will know the best place to contact) or **Patan Hospital** in Lagankhel, Patan, tel: 01-522278. This hospital is run by the United Mission to Nepal.

COMMUNICATION AND NEWS

Telecommunications and Postal Services

Main hotels have telephone, fax, email and mail facilities. International direct dial telephone communications are satellite-linked and excellent. The country code is 977 and the Kathmandu area code is 1. To call abroad, dial the international access code 00, then the country code: Australia (61); France (33); Germany (49); Japan (81); Netherlands (31); Spain (34); UK (44); and US and Canada (1). Sprint, AT&T and MCI cards cannot be used here.

If you need to seek assistance, dial 186 for the international operator, 187 for calls to India, 180 for internal trunk calls and 197 for enquiries.

Fax facilities are available in most hotels and offices. Public services in business centres are available in Thamel and Durbar Marg. There are now numerous cybercafés in Thamel and sending and receiving email is easy and cheap.

The mail service is less reliable so avoid having people send you letters during your visit. Mail cards or letters at your hotel or at the General Post Office (tel: 01-227499) at the junction of Kantipath and Kicha-Pokhari.

Media

There are several newspapers in English and dozens in Nepali. The *Kathmandu Post* and the *Rising Nepal* are the two English-language dailies, both giving thin coverage of world news. Two weeklies, *The Independent* (published on Wednesdays) and *People's Review* are also available.

The International Herald Tribune can be found one day late at newsstands and available weekly are *Time*, *Newsweek*, the *Far Eastern Economic Review*, *Asiaweek* and *India Today*.

Useful magazines include the *Nepal Traveller* and *Traveller's Nepal,* both handed out free. Look out also for the excellent, environmentally-oriented *Himal* monthly magazine on South Asia.

Radio Nepal broadcasts two news bulletins in English daily at 8am and 8pm. A range of channels including CNN, BBC and StarTV is now available on satellite TV. Check the programmes daily in the *Rising Nepal* and bring a shortwave radio if you are addicted to international news.

SPECIAL INFORMATION
Nepali Language

There are as many tongues spoken in Nepal as there are races and almost as many dialects as there are valleys. The official language, Nepali, is derived from Pahori, an Indian language related to Hindi and uses the same writing system, Devanagari. Nepali has also borrowed heavily from Sanskrit, an ancient scholarly language which has survived (like Latin) as a religious medium. Newari, the unique ancient language of the Newar people predominant in the Kathmandu Valley, uses three different alphabets and is the richest in literature and poetry.

In northern Nepal, the Tibetan language remains widespread and is the basis of dialects such as Sherpa and Thakali. English is widely spoken and understood, especially in government and tourism-related circles.

SPORTS

Paradoxically, skiing is out of the question in Nepal, although a few mountaineering expeditions attempt it. The steepness of slopes and high snow line and altitude make skiing impractical. White water rafting, on the other hand, is becoming very popular *(see page 61).* The water is generally at its highest after the June to September monsoon and lowest in February to March.

Nepal's first bungee jump opened in 1999, located 160 metres (525 ft) over the Bhote Koshi gorge, just 5 km (3 miles) from the Tibetan border and operated by **Last Resort Adventures**. Rock climbing, canyoning and mountain biking is available from the **Borderland Adventure Centre** (contact them in Taopani, Kathmandu, tel: 01-425836, fax: 01-435207, email: info@borderlands.net).

If planning on mountain biking, bring with you all the tools you will need for maintenance and repair, as these aren't readily available in Nepal. Bring a 'portager' for carrying the bike over the rougher ground.

The five-star hotels all have swimming pools, tennis courts and some have health clubs. Temporary members are also welcome at the **Royal Nepal Golf Club** (tel: 01-472836) near the airport.

In general, however, sports facilities are very limited for visitors. Leisure is a concept unfamiliar to Nepalis who spend their spare time tending to family and religious commitments.

USEFUL INFORMATION (01)
Key Telephone Numbers

Police Emergency	100
Ambulance	211959
	228094
Patan Hospital	522278
Teaching Hospital	412808
CIWEC Clinic	228531
Nepal International Clinic	435357
Fire Brigade	101
Telephone Enquiry	197
International Operator	186

Foreign Missions and Consulates in Kathmandu

AUSTRALIA
Bansbari, tel: 371678, fax: 371533
BANGLADESH
Naxal, tel: 414943
BURMA (MYANMAR)
Chakrapat, tel: 521788, fax: 523402
CANADA
Lazimpat, tel: 415193, fax: 410422
CHINA
Baluwatar, tel: 411740, fax: 414045
INDIA
Lainchaur, tel: 410900, fax: 413132
ISRAEL
Lazimpat, tel: 411811, fax: 413920
NEW ZEALAND
Dilli Bazaar, tel: 412436, fax: 414750
PAKISTAN

Maharajganj, tel: 374024, fax: 374012
THAILAND
Bansbari, tel: 371410, fax: 371409
UNITED KINGDOM
Lainchaur, tel: 414588, fax: 411789
USA
Pani Pokhari, tel: 411179, fax: 419963

Credit Card Offices

AMERICAN EXPRESS
Durbar Marg, tel: 226152; fax: 226152
MASTERCARD AND VISA
c/o Nepal Grindlays Bank, Kantipath
tel: 254002; fax: 226762

International Organisations

BRITISH COUNCIL
Kantipath, tel: 221305, fax: 224076
FRENCH CULTURAL CENTRE
Thapathali, tel: 241163, fax: 226152
GOETHE INSTITUTE
Sundhara, tel: 250871
UNITED NATIONS
Pulchok, tel: 523200, fax: 523991

International Airlines

AIR CANADA
Durbar Marg, tel: 222838
AIR FRANCE
Durbar Marg, tel: 223339
AIR INDIA
Hattisar, tel: 415637
AUSTRIAN AIRLINES
Kamaladi, tel: 2233171, fax: 241506
BIMAN BANGLADESH
Naxaul, tel: 434740, fax: 434869
BRITISH AIRWAYS
Durbar Marg, tel: 222266, fax: 226611
CATHAY PACIFIC
Kantipath, tel: 411725
CHINA SOUTHWEST AIRLINES
Kamaladi, tel: 419770, fax: 416541
DRUK AIR
Durbar Marg, tel: 255166, fax: 227229
GULF AIR
Hattisar, tel: 430456, fax: 435301
INDIAN AIRLINES
Kamal Pokhari, tel: 414596, fax: 419649
JAPAN AIRLINES
Durbar Marg, tel: 222838
LUFTHANSA
Durbar Marg, tel: 223052, fax: 221900
NORTHWEST ORIENT AIRLINES
Lekhnath Marg, tel: 418389

PAKISTAN INTERNATIONAL
Durbar Marg, tel: 223102
QANTAS
Durbar Marg, tel: 220245
ROYAL NEPAL
New Road, tel: 220757, fax: 225348
SINGAPORE AIRLINES
Durbar Marg, tel: 220759, fax: 226795
SWISSAIR
Hattisar, tel: 434607, fax: 434570
THAI INTERNATIONAL
Durbar Marg, tel: 221316, fax: 221130
TRANSAVIA
Heritage Plaza, Kamaladi, tel: 247215, fax: 244484

Domestic Airlines

BUDDHA AIR
Hattisar, tel: 437677, fax: 437025, email: buddhaair@buddhaair.co
DYNASTY AVIATION
Lazimpat, tel: 410090, fax: 414627
GORKHA AIRLINES
Hattisar, tel: 436576, fax: 435430, email: gorkha@mos.com.np

Elephant safari

LUMBINI AIRWAYS
Min Bhawan, tel: 482728, fax: 483380, email: lumbini@resv.wlink.com.np
NECON AIR
Kalimati, tel: 473860, fax: 471679, email: reservation@necon.mos.com.np
YETI AIRLINES
Lazimpat, tel: 421215, fax: 420766

Travel Agencies

ANNAPURNA TRAVELS & TOURS
Durbar Marg, tel: 223530, fax: 222966, email: navraj@mos.com.np
EVEREST EXPRESS
Durbar Marg, tel: 220759, fax: 226795, email: info@everest-express.com.np
KATHMANDU TRAVELS & TOURS
Battisputali, tel: 471577, fax: 471379, email: dwarika@mos.com.np
MARCO POLO
Kamaladi, tel: 247215, fax: 244484, email: marco@polo.col.com.np
NATRAJ TOURS & TRAVELS
Ghantaghar, tel: 222906, fax: 227372, email: natraj@vishnu.ccsl.com.np
TIBET TRAVELS & TOURS
Tridevi Marg, tel: 418363, fax: 426546, email: sitaktm@sitanep.mos.com.np
YETI TRAVELS
Durbar Marg, tel: 221234, fax: 226152, email: yeti@vishnu.ccsl.com.np

Adventure Travel Agencies

BALLOON SUNRISE NEPAL
Lazimpat, tel: 424131; fax 424157, email: balloon@sunrise.mos.com.np
AVIA CLUB NEPAL
Dubar Marg, tel: 412830, fax: 415266, email: nepal@aviaclub.mos.com.np
LAST RESORT ADVENTURES
Thamel, tel: 439526, fax: 414765, email: rivers@ultimate.wlink.com.np
THE BORDERLAND ADVENTURE CENTRE
Barhabise, Tatopani, tel: 425836, fax: 435207, email: info@borderlands.net

Trekking Agencies

AMA DABLAM ADVENTURE GROUP
Kamal Pokhari, tel: 414644, fax: 416029, email: sales@amadablam.wlink.com.np
ASIAN TREKKING
Tridevi Marg, tel: 415506, fax: 411878, email: asianadv@mos.com.np
HIMALAYAN JOURNEYS
Kantipath, tel: 226138, fax: 227068, email: hjtrek@mos.com.np
INTERNATIONAL TREKKERS
Chabahil, tel: 371397, fax: 371561, email: nepal@intrek.wlink.com.np
MALLA TREKS
Lainchaur, tel: 410089, fax: 423143, email: surendra@malla.trk.mos.com.np
MOUNTAIN TRAVEL NEPAL

Lazimpat, tel: 411225, fax: 414075, email: info@tigermountain.com
SHERPA COOPERATIVE TREKKING
Durbar Marg, tel: 224068, fax: 227983, email: sherpaco@trekk.mos.com.np
SHERPA TREKKING SERVICE
Kamaladi, tel: 220243, fax: 227243, email: lamasts@wlink.com.np
THAMSERKU TREKKING AND TRAVEL
Basundhara, tel: 354491, fax: 354323, email: serku@vishnu.ccsl.com.np

River Trip Specialists

GREAT HIMALAYAN RIVERS
Lazimpat, tel: 410937; fax 226608, email: gha@mos.com.np
HIMALAYAN RIVER EXPLORATION
Lazimpat, tel: 411225; fax 414075, email: info@tigermountain.com
WHITE MAGIC
Jyatha, tel: 253225; fax 249885, email: wmagic@wlink.com.np
ULTIMATE DESCENTS INTERNATIONAL
Thamel, tel: 439526; fax 414765, email: rivers@ultimate.wlink.com.np

FURTHER READING

There are a number of excellent book-shops in Kathmandu, where you will find books on the region. They include **Mandala Book Point** and **Himalayan Booksellers** in Kantipath and **Pilgrims Book Centre** in the depths of Thamel.

General

Hagen, Toni. *Nepal: The Kingdom in the Himalayas*. Berne: Kummerly and Frey, 1996. Geographical study with many photos and maps. Hagen, who spent eight years surveying Nepal, was one of the first foreigners to travel widely in the country.

Choegyal, Lisa. *Insight Guide: Nepal*. Apa Publications, Singapore, 1991 (updated 2000). Complete coverage of trekking, climbing, national parks, the Terai and Kathmandu Valley.

Peissel, Michel. *Tiger for Breakfast*. Hodder, London, 1966. The story of Boris Lissanevitch, who came to Kathmandu in 1951 and opened the first hotel, the Royal.

Suyin, Han. *The Mountain is Young*.

Jonathon Cape, London, 1958. Novel set in Nepal in the 1950s.

People, Art and Culture

Anderson, Mary M. *Festivals of Nepal.* George Allen & Unwin, London, 1971.

Aran, Lydia. *The Art of Nepal.* Shahayogi Prakashan, Kathmandu, 1978. Mostly about the Kathmandu Valley with an accent on religion.

Bista, Dor Bahadur. *People of Nepal.* Ratna Pustak Bhandar, Kathmandu, 1974. Classic survey.

Natural History

Fleming, R.L. Sr, R.L. Fleming Jr and L.S. Bangdel. *Birds of Nepal.* Avalok, Kathmandu, 1979. Definitive work, good illustrations.

Inskipp, Carol. *A Birdwatcher's Guide to Nepal.* Bird Watchers Guides, England, 1988. Excellent and helpful guide.

McDougal, Charles. *The Face of the Tiger.* Rivington Books and Andre Deutsch, London, 1977. Classic work on the tiger by the Wildlife Director of Tiger Tops.

Polunin, Oleg and Stainton, Adam. *Concise Flowers of the Himalaya.* Oxford University Press, New Delhi, 1987. A standard work with beautiful illustrations.

Smith, Colin. *Butterflies of Nepal (Central Himalaya).* Teopress, Bangkok, 1989. Scholarly standard work.

Storrs, Adrian & Jimmy. *Enjoy Trees: A simple guide to some of the shrubs found in Nepal.* Sahayogi Press, Kathmandu, 1987. Useful and practical handbook.

Trekking

Bezruschka, Stephen. *A Guide to Trekking in Nepal.* The Mountaineers, Seattle, 1997. Probably the best trekking guide. For individual treks in the Everest, Annapurna and Langtang regions. Look out for the Trailblazer series of guidebooks.

Hillary, Sir Edmund. *Insight Topic: Sagarmatha.* Apa, Singapore 1992. Unique collection of stunning photographs of the Everest collected as a fund-raising classic for the Himalayan Trust.

O'Connor, Bill. *The Trekking Peaks of Nepal.* Seattle: Cloudcap Press 1989 and England: Crowood Press. Useful maps.

Kathmandu bookstore front

Websites on Nepal

south-asia.com has a section on Nepal.

www.info-nepal.com, the Nepal home page, provides links to several directories on Nepal.

Many guesthouses, magazines and local trekking companies advertise on the popular **www.catmando.com**.

GLOSSARY

A

Ananda	Buddha's chief disciple.
Ananta	A huge snake whose coils created Vishnu's bed.
arak	A whisky fermented from potatoes or grain.
Asadh	The third month of the Nepalese year.
Ashwin	The sixth month of the Nepalese year.
Ashta Matrikas	The eight mother goddesses said to attend on Shiva.
Avalokiteshwara	A *bodhisattva* regarded as the god of mercy in Mahayana Buddhist tradition, and as the compassionate Machhendra in Nepal.
avatar	An incarnation of a deity on earth.

B

bahal	A two-storey Buddhist monastery enclosing a courtyard.
bahil	A Buddhist monastery, smaller and simpler than a *bahal*.

Kathmandu building facade

	mantras or holy scriptures.
chhang	A potent mountain beer of fermented grain, usually barley.
chhetri	The Hindu warrior caste, second in status only to *brahmans*.
chiya	Nepalese tea, brewed together with milk, sugar and spices.
chorten	A small Buddhist shrine usually in high mountain regions.
chowk	A palace or public courtyard.
crore	A unit of counting equal to 10 million.

D – F

Dalai Lama	The reincarnate high priest of Tibetan Buddhism and political leader of Tibetans around the world.
Dattatraya	A syncretistic deity variously worshipped as an incarnation of Vishnu, a teacher of Shiva, or a cousin of the Buddha.
Devi	(or *Maha Devi*) 'The great goddess'. Shiva's *shakti* in her many forms.
dhal	A lentil soup.
Dharma	Buddhist doctrine. Literally 'the path'.
dharmasala	A public rest house for travellers and pilgrims.
doko	A basket, often carried on the head by means of a strap.
dorje	A ritual sceptre or thunderbolt, symbol of the Absolute to Tantric Buddhists (also *vajra*).
Durga	Shiva's *shakti* in one of her most awesome forms.
dyochhen	A house enshrining protective Tantric deities and used for common worship.

G – H

gaine	A wandering, begging minstrel.

Baisakh	First month of the Nepalese year.
Bajra Jogini	A Tantric goddess.
betel	A stimulating mixture of areca nut and white lime, wrapped in a betel leaf and chewed.
Bhadra	The fifth month of the Nepalese year.
Bhagavad-Gita	The most important Hindu religious scripture, in which the god Krishna spells out the importance of duty. It is contained in the *Mahabharata*.
Bhairav	The god Shiva in his most terrifying form.
Bhimsen	A deity worshipped for his strength and courage.
bodhisattva	In Mahayana tradition, a person who has attained the enlightened level of Buddhahood, but has chosen to remain on earth to teach until others are enlightened.
Bon	The pre-Buddhist religion of Tibet, incorporating animism and sorcery.
Brahma	In Hindu mythology, the god of creation.
brahman	The highest Hindu caste, originally of priests.

C

Chaitra	The 12th and last month of the Nepalese year.
chaitya	A small stupa, sometimes containing a Buddhist relic, but usually holding

Ganesh	The elephant-headed son of Shiva and Parvati. He is worshipped as the god of good luck and the remover of obstacles.
Garuda	A mythical eagle, half human. The vehicle of Vishnu.
Gautama Buddha	The historical Buddha, born in Lumbini in the 6th century BC.
ghat	A riverside platform for bathing and cremation.
gompa	Tibetan Buddhist monastery.
Gorakhnath	Historically, an 11th-century yogi who founded a Shaivite cult; now popularly regarded as an incarnation of Shiva.
guthi	A communal Newar brotherhood, serving the purpose of mutual support for members and their extended families.
Hanuman	A deified monkey. Hero of the *Ramayana* epic, he is believed to bring success to armies.
hiti	A water conduit; a bath or tank with water spouts.

I – J

Indra	The god of rain.
Jagannath	Krishna, worshipped as 'Lord of the World'.
jatra	Festival.
Jestha	The second month of the Nepalese year.
jhankri	A shahman or sorcerer.
jogini	A mystical goddess.
jyapu	Newar farmer caste.

K

Kali	Shiva *shakti* in her most terrifying form.
karma	The cause and effect chain of actions, good and bad, from one life to the next.
Kartik	The seventh month of the Nepalese year.
khukhri	A traditional knife, long and curved, best known as the weapons of Gurkha soldiers.
Krishna	The eighth incarnation of Vishnu, worshipped for his activities on earth.
kumari	A young virgin regarded as a living goddess in Kathmandu Valley towns.

L

lakh	A unit equal to 100,000.
Lakshmi	The goddess of wealth and consort of Vishnu.
lama	A Tibetan Buddhist priest.
lingum	A symbolic male phallus, generally associated with Shiva; (plural:*linga*).

M

Machhendra	The guardian god of the Kathmandu Valley, guarantor of rain and plenty, who is enshrined as the Rato (Red) Machhendra in Patan and the Seto (White) Machhendra in Kathmandu.
Magh	The 10th month of the Nepalese year.
Mahabharata	An important Hindu epic.
Mahayana	A form of Buddhism prevalent in East Asia, Tibet and Nepal.
Maitreya	The future Buddha.
mandala	A sacred diagram envisioned by Tibetan Buddhists as an aid to meditation.
mandap	A roofless Tantric shrine made of brick or wood.
mani	a wall or pile of stones with Buddhist *mantra* carved on them.
Manjushri	The legendary Buddhist patriarch of the Kathmandu Valley, now often regarded as the god of learning.
mantra	Sacred syllables chanted during meditation by Buddhists.
Marga	The eighth month of the Nepalese year.

math	A Hindu priest's house.
munja	The sacred thread worn by Brahman and Chettri males from the time of puberty.

N

naga	Snake, especially a legendary or a deified serpent.
namaste	A very common word of greeting, often translated as: 'I salute all divine qualities in you'.
Nandi	A bull, Shiva's vehicle and a symbol of fecundity.
Narayan	Vishnu represented as the creator of life.
nath	Literally, 'place'.
nirvana	Extinction of self, the goal of meditation.

P

panchayat	The old government system consisting of elected councils at local, regional and national levels.
Parvati	Shiva's consort, displaying both serene and fearful aspects.
pashmina	A shawl or blanket made of fine goat's wool.
Pashupati	Shiva in his aspect as 'Lord of the Beasts'. Symbolised by the *lingum*, he is believed to bring fecundity.
path	A small raised platform which provides shelter for travellers on important routes and intersections.
paubha	Traditional Newari painting, usually religious in motif.
Paush	The ninth month of the Nepalese year.
pokhari	A large tank.
Phalgun	The 11th month of the Nepalese year.
puja	Ritual offerings to the gods.

R

rakshi	A homemade wheat or rice liquor.
Rama	The seventh incarnation of Vishnu. A prince of the *Ramayana* epic.
Ramayana	The most widely known Hindu legend, in which Rama, with the aid of Hanuman and Garuda, rescues his wife, Sita, from the demon king Rawana.
Rawana	The anti-hero of the *Ramayana*.
rimpoche	The abbot of a Tibetan Buddhist monastery.

S

sadhu	A Hindu mendicant.
sanyasin	A religious ascetic who has renounced his ties to society.
Saraswati	Brahma's consort, worshipped in Nepal as the Hindu goddess of learning.
satal	A pilgrim's house.
shakti	Shiva's consort. Literally, the dynamic element in the male-female relationship, and the female aspect of the Tantric Absolute.
shikhara	A brick or stone temple of geometrical shape with a tall central spire.
Shitala Mai	A former ogress who became protector of children, worshipped at Swayambhunath.
Shiva	The most awesome of Hindu gods. He destroys all things, good as well as evil, allowing new creation to take shape.
Shrawan	The fourth month of the Nepalese year.
Sita	Rama's wife, heroine of the *Ramayana* epic.
stupa	A bell-shaped relic chamber.
sundhara	A fountain with a golden spout.

Surjya	The sun god, often identified with Vishnu.
suttee	Former practise of immolating widows on their husband's funeral pyres.

T – U

Taleju Bhawani	The Nepalese goddess, originally a South Indian deity; an aspect of Devi.
Tara	Historically a Nepalese princess now deified by Buddhists and Hindus.
Terai	The Nepalese lowland region.
thangka	Religious scroll painting.
tika	A vermilion powder applied by Hindus to the forehead as a symbol of the presence of the divine.
tol	A street.
topi	Traditional Nepalese cap.
torana	Decorative carved crest over the door of a sanctum, with the figure of the deity at its centre.

V – Z

vajra	In Tantric Buddhism, a ritual thunderbolt or curved sceptre symbolising the Absolute. It also represents power and male energy (also *dorje*).
vihara	A Buddhist monastery, encompassing a *bahal* and a *bahil*.
Vishnu	One of the Hindu trinity, a god who preserves life and world itself. In Nepal, he is most commonly represented as Narayan.
yoni	A hole in a stone symbolising the female sexual aspect. Usually seen together with a *lingum*.

ACKNOWLEDGMENTS

Cover	**Hugh Sitton/Stone**
Backcover	**Chris Caldicott**
3, 4, 27, 28, 29, 31, 37, 39, 40, 43, 44, 46, 51, 55, 72, 75, 84, 86, 90, 92T, 93T	**Alain Evrard**
82	**Belinda Edwards**
47	**Craig Lovell**
26	**David Messent**
62	**Denise Tackett**
52	**Frances Klatzel**
33, 53, 54, 59, 65, 66, 67T, 68, 85	**Galen Rowell**
78, 81	**Frances Higgins**
17, 87	**Jean Kugler**
61	**Jennifer Read**
35, 50, 69, 71, 80T, 88	**Jock Montogomery**
16	**Julian Cowan**
22	**K. Debnick**
43	**Kevin Bubriski**
14, 15, 19, 57, 79, 80B, 83T, 94	**Lisa Choegyal**
67B	**Nik Wheeler**
6, 43B	**Sanu Bajracharya**
34, 58, 70, 82	**Wendy Brewer Lama**
27T, 73, 74	**W.D. Andreae**
6/7	**Galen Rowell**
10/11	**Thomas Laird**
Handwriting	**V. Barl**
Maps	**Berndtson & Berndtson**
Cover Design	**Carlotta Junger and Tanvir Virdee**

U – V

W – Z

The travel guides that replace a tour guide - now better than ever with more listings and a fresh new design

INSIGHT
Pocket Guides

Insight Pocket Guides pioneered a new approach to guidebooks, introducing the concept of the authors as "local hosts" who would provide readers with personal recommendations, just as they would give honest advice to a friend who came to stay. They also included a full-size pull-out map. Now, to cope with the needs of the 21st century, new editions in this growing series are being given a new look to make them more practical to use, and restaurant and hotel listings have been greatly expanded.

☆INSIGHT GUIDES

The world's largest collection of visual travel guides

Now in association with

Notes